The Play
Solution

The Play Solution

HOW TO PUT THE FUN AND EXCITEMENT

BACK INTO YOUR RELATIONSHIP

Jeanette C. Lauer, Ph.D.
Robert H. Lauer, Ph.D.

Contemporary Books

Chicago   New York   San Francisco   Lisbon   London   Madrid   Mexico City
Milan   New Delhi   San Juan   Seoul   Singapore   Sydney   Toronto

Library of Congress Cataloging-in-Publication Data

Lauer, Jeanette C.
    The play solution : how to put the fun and excitement back into your
relationship / Jeanette C. Lauer and Robert H. Lauer.
       p.   cm.
    ISBN 0-07-139010-3 (alk. paper)
    1. Couples.   2. Play.   3. Man-woman relationships.
    4. Intimacy (Psychology)   I. Title: How to put the fun and excitement
back into your relationship   II. Lauer, Robert H.   III. Title.

HQ801.L325   2002
305.3—dc21   2002276814

Contemporary Books

A Division of The McGraw·Hill Companies

1 2 3 4 5 6 7 8 9 0   DOC/DOC   1 0 9 8 7 6 5 4 3 2

ISBN 0-07-139010-3

McGraw-Hill books are available at special quantity discounts to use as premiums
and sales promotions, or for use in corporate training programs. For more
information, please write to the Director of Special Sales, Professional Publishing,
McGraw-Hill, Two Penn Plaza, New York, NY 10121-2298. Or contact your local
bookstore.

This book is printed on acid-free paper.

To our playful partners in the game of life:
Jon, Kathy, Julie, Jeffrey, Kate, Jeff, Krista, Benjamin,
David, and John Robert

Contents

Preface

YOU'VE HEARD IT said many times—perhaps too many times: "You have to work at a relationship." That's true. Yet if a relationship is nothing but work, it's probably not really working for you. An intimate relationship—whether you're dating, living together, engaged, or married—should be joy as well as work. And for that, you need play.

That's what this book is all about—how to have a playful relationship. First a disclaimer: We don't view play as some kind of relational cure-all, an elixir that guarantees a lasting and satisfying relationship. After all, how much contact do you still have with your childhood playmates? Given the limitations, however, we do claim that building a lasting and fulfilling adult relationship demands a measure of play.

This is a practical book. It's also a serious one; the stability and satisfaction of your relationship is not to be taken lightly. However, it's also a playful book, offering you and your partner many ideas and exercises about how to become a more playful couple. In addition to suggestions throughout the chapters, we have play-enhancing exercises for you at the end of each chapter. Don't neglect them. Remember, it's not just *knowing* about couple play but *engaging* in it that adds sizzle to your relationship.

We are grateful to our agent, Andrea Pedolsky, and our editor, Judith McCarthy, for their support of this project. We are also indebted to the numerous couples we have worked with. They have taught us why it's important to play, as well as how to (and how not to) play. Their influence is seen on every page.

1

How Much Fun Are You Having?

We were chatting with a friend in a restaurant when we recognized a couple at another table. Our friend remarked with a sigh that the couple had "a to-die-for marriage." He hastened to add that his own marriage was good, but said theirs was "off the charts" in terms of how much they seemed to enjoy each other.

We agreed with his assessment, and thought of another couple who had anything but a to-die-for marriage. Tanya and Jack had attended a marriage enrichment seminar where we gave couples a variety of assignments. One assignment was to come up with a list of fun and exciting things they'd like to do together over the next five years. The list was to include only those things that both partners would enjoy. "Use your imagination," we urged them, "and don't throw away an idea at this point just because you think it's impractical."

During the break that followed, we came across Jack, who was alone at the moment. "How did the assignment go?" we asked. He shook his head and replied grimly, "Tanya doesn't have an imaginative bone in her body. Not a single one!"

These two couples represent the extremes. How do you and your partner compare? Are you more like the couple with the to-die-for relationship, or more like the couple whose relationship is mired in deadly boredom? Or are you somewhere in between? How much do you enjoy each other? How much fun do you have together? Your answers are important because they provide crucial clues to your prospects for a lasting and satisfying relationship.

A Relationship Is Like a Rose Garden

Having spent many years cultivating our own relationship and observing human behavior, we can say with confidence that all couples have times of beauty and enjoyment (when the roses are in glorious bloom), times of toil and routine (when countless hours are spent cultivating, feeding, and weeding), and times of struggle and pain (when the thorns and garden pests finally get you).

What would you do if the rosebushes you diligently planted and tended yielded little more than thorns or mildew? You'd likely dig them up and plant marigolds instead. It's the same with relationships. If your relationship brings more pain and trouble than anything else, it probably won't last. Even if it does last, it will bring little joy. So we recommend that you keep the garden of your relationship in flowering shape by treating it to an ample dose of play. We'll explore the many benefits of couple play in the next chapter, but here we want to be clear about what we mean by couple play and underscore its importance for keeping your relationship strong and satisfying.

A Rose Garden Is a Hobby . . . or Not

We know a couple who maintain a rose garden as a hobby. They are passionate about their roses and treasure every moment they spend on their hobby. We also once had a rose garden, but we never viewed it as a hobby. It was a chore. To be sure, it was a chore that sometimes produced beautiful flowers, but it was still a chore. And we never reached a point where we thought of it in any other way.

In the same way, an activity can be enjoyable couple play for some people but something entirely different for others. For example, Seth and Jenna, an engaged couple, decided to take up golf together. Jenna had played golf since she was a teenager. She thoroughly enjoyed the game and had a real aptitude for it. Seth had never been on a golf course. Jenna assured him that she'd teach him the fundamentals and that they'd have a great time. But after she told him for the thirteenth time (and they were only on the third hole) to "keep your head down" when he drove the ball, he snapped back, "You don't have to keep saying that. I know it. I just have to work at it a little more." By the end of the day, they were both exhausted. Nevertheless, they persisted. On their fifth outing, Seth drove the ball well on a couple of holes and his putting improved markedly. Curiously, Jenna felt a bit challenged by his progress. She began to concentrate more on her own game and snicker at his mistakes. As a result, Seth felt challenged and embarked on a crusade—to improve at the game until he could beat Jenna.

Were Seth and Jenna engaged in couple play? Not at all. Their competition had reached the point where golf wasn't play for either of them. Think about their situation in terms of the definition of play set forth by psychologist Paul Roberts, who writes that true play "is pure pleasure, an activity undertaken solely for enjoyment. Play is intense, absorbing, and invigorating. It can override consciousness, displace anger, anxiety, and fear."[1]

When you play, the activity is its own reward. You don't need, like Seth, to have a goal of proving yourself better than someone else. When you play, you gain pleasure from the experience. Seth and Jenna felt more exhaustion and frustration than pleasure from their outings on the golf course. When you play, you find the experience absorbing—other matters are blocked out of your consciousness and you are able to escape from the everyday cares and struggles of your life. Seth and Jenna were more absorbed in outperforming the other than in the experience of playing. He was determined to improve his game until he was better than Jenna, and she was concerned that Seth would eventually outplay her. They were clearly not engaged in couple play. Rather, they were competing, working at the grim task of trying to outdo each other. Their attempt at play had turned into a deadly serious enterprise.

Serious, Yes; Deadly Serious, No

Couple play is a serious matter in the sense that it is inextricably tied up with the well-being of your relationship. But don't, like Seth and Jenna, let this serious matter become a deadly serious activity. If you let your relationship become deadly serious, it will die. We have asked many people about what qualities they value in a partner, and we've yet to have a person tell us, "I'm looking for someone who is dull, humorless, and boring." Rather, we have heard statements like these:

- "He makes me laugh."
- "We enjoy being with each other."
- "She's the most interesting, exciting person I know."
- "We have great times together."

When you can't say something like this about your partner, your relationship is in trouble. Consider the case of Patricia, who was on the verge of marriage when her "textbook" romance came to a screeching halt:

"I met Jason at work. He's a financial planner like me, so we had something in common from the start. A week after we first met, we had our first date. And it wasn't long until we were involved in an exclusive relationship."

Patricia knew from the beginning that Jason was a serious fellow. When they were out together, he'd talk a lot about problems at work, as well as difficulties he had in a previous marriage. He had been briefly married several years earlier and was determined never again to go through the trauma of a breakup. Unfortunately, Jason's seriousness didn't end there; it seemed to carry over to everything else in his life. On more than one occasion, Patricia thought to herself that he needed to lighten up, and sometimes she would even say to him in a teasing way, "Don't be so serious."

They had been dating for six months when Jason asked her to marry him. Much to her surprise, Patricia told him she'd need a few days before she could give him an answer:

"It was strange, because I'd been waiting for this moment. I'd always wanted to get married and have a family. And Jason and I seemed so well matched. We had a textbook relationship—on paper we were perfectly suited to each other. We shared the same interests, the same work, similar family and church background. But something made me hesitate.

"I couldn't quite put my finger on the problem until I had lunch the next day with my best friend. I wanted to talk to her about Jason's proposal. But before I ever got around to it, we were both laughing over something that had happened to her that morning. It was like a revelation from heaven. I suddenly realized why I couldn't accept Jason's proposal. Jason and I seldom laughed together like my friend and I did. We were never silly together. In fact, I had to admit that I usually felt uptight when I was with him. I knew right then and there that I couldn't marry someone who made me feel serious and uneasy so much of the time."

Play Is Your Sunshine

There's something else about a rose garden. It won't flourish without the life-giving light of the sun. The same is true in a relationship; play is the sunshine necessary for its growth. The importance of play was underscored for us several years ago when we studied couples in long-term marriages.[2] The study began one day when we were running together (which, by the way, we have found to be a good way to connect with each other and to generate ideas). We were discussing the breakup of a couple we knew and lamenting the fact that so many of our friends and acquaintances had divorced. Is there something wrong with us, we wondered, that we're still together? We quickly rejected that possibility but began to speculate on why our relationship had lasted when others around us were failing. We decided to find out.

We searched the professional literature and found numerous studies about why people break up, but little on what holds couples together. Moreover, materials written about what makes relationships last were largely inferences drawn from couples who had broken up. So we decided to investigate the topic by looking at healthy rather than troubled relationships, asking what factors kept those relationships stable and fulfilling. To answer the question, we interviewed three hundred couples who had been married anywhere from fifteen to sixty-one years and who said they were happy in their relationship.

One of our findings was that both the husbands and wives (they were interviewed separately) agreed on the importance of play, including humor, in their relationship. In fact, they ranked it above sex in terms of its importance! As a husband of twenty-six years put it, "Laughter is a steady diet here. Our kids are funny and so is most of life. One needs a satiric eye in order to survive."

Maria, married fifteen years, told about a critical time in her marriage when it reached the ten-year point:

"Todd, my husband, was going great guns in his career. But he was doing it at the expense of me and our two kids. He was spending long hours in his office and was still absorbed in his work when he came home. You could tell that his mind was somewhere else even when he was with us.

"It came to a climax one day when I was so angry that I clammed up. He finally noticed my silence and asked me what was wrong. I told him I thought our marriage was a shambles and that I felt like he was neglecting us. I let him know that he wasn't fun to be around anymore and that things had to change if we were going to stay together."

Maria's statement startled Todd. But he acknowledged that she was right and that he wanted to get their relationship back on track. Together they worked on ways to help him cut back on the amount of time he worked, to leave his work at the office, and to once again be the engaged, playful person he was in the early years of their marriage:

"I'm delighted to say that things really changed, and Todd gets most of the credit. Except for the rare occasion, he leaves his work at the office. Instead of dreading his homecoming, we look forward to it. He no longer stalks into the house without a word. He spends time romping with the kids. He takes time to linger over coffee with me after dinner. And we even find time for a date now and then. Our marriage is better than ever!"

Three Rules of Couple Play

Playless relationships, as Maria found out, can easily turn into broken relationships. As we prefer to put it, the couple that plays together is more likely to stay together. Please note that the key word here is *together*. We're not talking about you doing your thing while your partner does his or her thing. You, of course, need a certain amount of individual play, but you also need couple play. And to engage in couple play, you need to follow a few simple rules.

Rule One: If It's Work, It Isn't Couple Play

Some play does involve an element of work—if you include learning the rules or honing skills as work. The test is whether what you're doing is more work than play or more play than work. And when you apply the test, keep in mind the characteristics of couple play. The activity should be, for both of you, pleasurable, absorbing, and done for its own sake.

In contrast, work for most people involves a certain amount of routine and drudgery. You probably have no choice; you work to support yourself and your dependents. Moreover, work typically entails competition. You compete with coworkers for promotions, pay increases, status, or perks. You compete with other companies. Or you compete to reach certain standards or professional goals you set for yourself.

Of course, many people enjoy their work—at least parts of it. We enjoy researching and writing. We enjoy the opportunities and income generated by our work. There are also things we don't enjoy—like doing rewrites and scanning proofs before they go to the printer. And we are certainly competing with other writers for attention and acceptance. But when we play, we don't care about these things. Sometimes a little friendly competition enters our play, but that's different from a determination to be the winner. In essence, when we play we just enjoy ourselves.

Keep in mind, for instance, that it *isn't* couple play if any of these are true:

- The basic reason for playing tennis with another couple is to cultivate a business relationship.
- Your mind is still on work while you are playing cards with your partner.
- You take a walk with your partner only to get him or her off your back so you can get back to work.
- You are more concerned with beating your partner than with having fun when you play a game together.
- Your bedroom renovation project is an exciting adventure for one of you but painful drudgery for the other.

In short, the more you bring elements of work into what you do, the less it is play. And the more you find an activity absorbing and intrinsically enjoyable, the more it is couple play—even if it's an activity that isn't usually thought of as play, like going to the grocery store together.

Rule Two: If You're Not Both Enjoying It, It Isn't Couple Play

Consider the following exchange between a husband (H) and wife (W):

W: Did you get the car taken care of today?

H: No, I didn't have time. I'll do it soon.

W: I don't want to worry about driving it.

H: What's to worry? It only needs a tuneup.

W: But what if I get stuck out somewhere?

H: You won't get stuck just because it needs a tuneup, you silly thing. You don't know a nut from a bolt when it comes to cars! Wait until I tell the guys at work about this one!

W: Yeah, that's right. Tell them how dumb your wife is.

H: Don't be so sensitive! I was just kidding.

The husband thought he was being playful, but his wife found his words hurtful. It's a common situation. We have dealt many times with couples in which one partner does or says things that he or she considers playful while the other partner considers them boring, irritating, insensitive, or hurtful. To paraphrase an old saying, one partner's joke may be the other partner's pain. And that's the essence of the second rule of couple play: It isn't play unless you're both enjoying it.

In response to Maria's warning that his preoccupation with work was threatening their marriage, Todd decided to do something to resurrect their relationship. One of the first things he came up with was to suggest that Maria accompany him to a convention he had to attend in Chicago. "We'll get a babysitter for the kids and have a couple of days all to ourselves," he proposed. Maria thought it sounded like a great idea. They wouldn't be that far from home in case an emergency arose with the children. Plus, there were all kinds of fun things to do in Chicago.

However, the trip didn't turn out as either of them had expected. Todd got tied up in meetings, and Maria spent much of the time wandering around the city alone. One of the two nights, they went to dinner with some people from Todd's firm, and business was the main topic of conversation. Maria was disappointed by the trip. "I know that the meeting was profitable for you," she complained to Todd, "but I would have had more fun at home." He was hurt and frustrated by Maria's reaction to the trip. "After all, I was trying, wasn't I?" he defensively responded. She agreed that his intentions were good. And they both agreed to find more pleasurable ways to play as a couple. Todd learned the second rule the hard way. He knew that in the future he'd have to think about whether something would be enjoyable for Maria as well as for him.

This isn't to say that you can't accommodate each other at times. For example, a wife told us that she accompanies her husband on his fishing trips not because she enjoys fishing but because he doesn't like to go alone. For him, it is a time of play. He thoroughly enjoys the experience. For her, there is some enjoyment in being with him and watching his exhilaration when he makes a catch. But she is glad when they return home. Such times are good for their relationship, but they are not couple play. Only he is playing; she is watching him play. Fortunately, they have other things they do for couple play. To reiterate, it's only couple play if you're both enjoying it, if you're both thinking of yourselves as playing.

Rule Three: If You Don't Feel Better About Yourselves and Your Relationship Afterward, It Isn't Couple Play

Let's go back to Seth and Jenna. Typically, Seth would feel frustrated after a game of golf, while Jenna would feel uneasy. Seth was frustrated because he wanted to progress more quickly so that he could beat Jenna. He had always viewed himself as inept at sports, and his perception that he was progressing slowly only reinforced this image. Jenna was perturbed because she believed her status as the more athletic of the two of them was being challenged. She valued her athletic ability. It was important to her self-esteem to be better at something than the multitalented Seth.

In other words, neither of them felt better about themselves after their golf games. Moreover, neither felt better about their relationship. They both realized that their attempt to play golf together strained rather than strengthened the bonds between them. Wisely, they eventually gave up the venture. Seth conceded that, for him, success at golf was not worth the effort. He decided that when Jenna played golf, he'd use the time to pursue some of his own interests.

For other couples, playing golf could have an opposite outcome. That's one of the challenges of couple play—to find the kind of activities that make you feel good about yourselves and your relationship. For instance, one of the ways we play is to take long walks together.

Walking makes us feel better physically and emotionally. It gives us an opportunity to chat and reconnect. Yet we have friends who view walking as a necessary nuisance and never as a form of play.

The point is, no activity will work for every couple. What you do together may not appeal to other couples. However, if it makes you feel better about yourselves and your relationship, it is couple play.

Confronting the Play Squelchers

We find that most people enthusiastically agree when we talk about the importance of play for relationships. Still, as the morose husband at our seminar illustrates, many relationships have little play in them. Or at least they lack sufficient play to maintain sizzle and stability. Why? What prevents couples from being playful? Here are a few reasons.

The Act Your Age Trap

"Act your age," a disgusted wife told her husband at a party. He was usually a quiet man. But he had gotten into the spirit of the festivities and had become the center of a lively group as he recounted stories from the research lab when he was in graduate school. People who had known him for years were delighted to discover that he could be so much fun. Only his wife was disturbed.

For the wife, "act your age" meant "You are an adult and a scientist with serious responsibilities. You shouldn't be acting silly and frivolous like a child." But why not? Why should it be that the average kindergartner laughs three hundred times a day while the average adult laughs seventeen times a day?[3] Apparently, growing up is no laughing matter for the average person. Is this necessary?

We're not saying that you should play as much as, or in the same way that, you did as a child. But don't get caught in the act your age trap. Don't let yourself be so inhibited that you're incapable of being spontaneous and playful. To be deadly serious as an adult is no more natural than to be deadly serious as a child.

We attended a Halloween costume party at a church and were intrigued by a mystery woman. She was dressed in a black blouse and tights. She wore a black beret, sunglasses, and a wig of long, lush blonde hair. It was a small congregation, but no one could identify the woman until the time came for unmasking. We were startled to see the seventy-eight-year-old matriarch of the congregation standing there with a grin on her face!

Did anyone think she was not acting her age? Was anyone embarrassed? Not in the least. We were delighted with her ability to be playful. She taught us all that play doesn't end when you become an adult, not even when you're seventy-eight years old.

The Tyranny of Schedules

"Are you staying busy?" is a common question we hear people ask each other. We've yet to hear someone reply, "Oh no, I have oodles of time on my hands. I just don't have enough to do to fill my days."

On the contrary, everyone seems busy. Nearly everyone we know echoes the complaint of Amanda, a lawyer, wife, and mother of three:

> "I am consistently overwhelmed by this heavy feeling that there is not enough time or enough of me to meet the demands of the day. My law firm expects me to work a ten-hour day, and my kids insist on my full attention once I get home. There is just nothing left for Rob and me."

As a dual-career couple who raised three children, we sympathize with Amanda. But we don't accept busyness—hers or anyone else's—as an excuse for not playing. We know too many busy couples who manage to keep their relationship vital by reserving time for play. You may have brief periods of time when your schedule crowds out play. But if it's a chronic condition, we have a question for you: Which is more important to you—your schedule or your relationship? You *do* have options. We simply won't accept your busy schedule as a justification for too little play in your relationship.

The Long Arm of Work

One of the rules, remember, is that if it's work it isn't play. Yet many people find it difficult to turn off the work mode and turn on the play mode. They bring the competitive spirit that drives them at work into their play and turn the play into work. A game becomes a battle to see who can win. A hobby becomes a way to earn extra money. Team sports offer an opportunity to make business contacts. And so on.

Even if you don't transfer your work habits into your play, technology has made the long arm of work even longer. Cell phones and E-mail keep you in the grasp of work wherever you go, particularly if you are in a career where you are expected to be available. One of the most relaxing vacations we ever had was on an island where we were relatively isolated. We didn't even receive a daily newspaper. We were astonished at how renewing it was to escape everything, from the ringing telephone to the daily glut of unsettling information in the media.

We've even started leaving our laptop at home when we vacation. We made this decision a couple of years ago when work "crises" followed us by E-mail wherever we went. The crises really didn't need immediate attention; moreover, we were powerless to handle them from a distance. The only thing we could do was worry. So now the laptop stays at home!

We still find the technology nettlesome, however, because we've been on trips or on an outing with friends and waited patiently (at least we *tried* to be forbearing) as they answered their cell phones or responded to their E-mail. When you travel for pleasure, we suggest that you send an E-mail to everyone in your address book informing them that you will not have access to your E-mail or to a cell phone on the dates you specify. Then go and enjoy yourselves.

So, How Much Fun Are You Having?

How much have the play squelchers squeezed out of your relationship? It's time to assess how you and your partner are doing. Each of you answer the following questionnaire separately. Take a sheet of paper, number it from 1 to 20, then respond to each of the statements in the "How Much Fun Are We Having?" questionnaire on page 16. Don't worry if you can't remember *exactly* how often you engage in some of the listed activities—just estimate as best you can.

When you have each finished, add up your scores. Your overall scores could range from 0 (Is your life really that grim?) to 80 (Did you cheat? No one can play that much!).

If you're wondering what's a passing score for a playful couple, the answer is: there's no such thing. The purpose of this questionnaire is not to compare your scores with those of others or to earn a grade on how well you're doing. Its purpose is fourfold. First, we want to sensitize you to the wide range of play activities. Are there items on the list that you've never done or not done recently? Think about trying or going back to some of them. Second, we want you to notice how frequently or infrequently you engage in various activities. How many activities, for example, did you rate as never, or rarely or infrequently, compared to the number you rated as frequently or daily?

Third, we want to sensitize you to the fact that you can engage in play on a daily basis. You probably won't take a trip or have playful sex every day. But what about things like flirting, joking, laughing together, and being silly? As we'll discuss in a later chapter, you can fit play into a lot of niches in any given day.

The final purpose of the questionnaire is to compare your scores with each other. Again, the point is not to see which of you is factu-

How Much Fun Are We Having?

Score each of the following statements according to the following scale:

0—Never
1—Rarely or infrequently
2—Occasionally
3—Frequently
4—Every day

1. We have special names we call each other.
2. My partner tells me jokes or funny stories.
3. We take trips that are fun.
4. At the end of the day, we can say we've had a good time.
5. We act silly with each other when we're alone.
6. We do impetuous things together.
7. We play games together.
8. We see and hear things that make us laugh together.
9. We play make-believe or pretend games.
10. We have playful sex together.
11. We flirt with each other.
12. We pursue a hobby together.
13. We engage in enjoyable physical activities together.
14. My partner says things that make me laugh.
15. My partner teases me in a playful way.
16. We do fun things with other couples.
17. We try new activities just for the fun of it.
18. My partner shows a good sense of humor.
19. We listen to music together.
20. My partner comes up with imaginative ways for us to have fun.

ally correct. Heaven forbid that a book about play should result in an argument! Rather, we want you to note how closely you agree on the amount of fun you're having. If your scores are far apart, talk about why you have such differing perceptions. Perhaps one of you feels more play deprived than the other. But don't worry at this point about your numbers. In Chapter 3, you'll have another chance to respond to other questionnaires that will help you to understand the type and quantity of play you need in your relationship.

So how much fun are you having? Look again at the questionnaire. Note the wide variety of play activities available to you. Also note that many of them require little or no money, planning, or intense effort. Play is not beyond the reach of any couple. All of us can play for keeps.

Play for Keeps

According to an old saying, every long journey begins with the first step. If your destination is to have a relationship that sizzles, you'll need to get there step by step. There will be obstacles in the way (the play squelchers). There will be times of crisis when play is the last thing on your mind. Don't let the obstacles or the times of crisis keep you from getting back on the path to becoming a more playful couple.

The questionnaire is a good place to begin. Select one of the items that you both agree is appealing and that you would like to do more often. Talk about how you can increase the frequency of that activity, keeping in mind that every step—even the small ones—brings you closer to your goal.

For example, some years ago we felt the need to travel more but felt hampered by various professional and family obligations. That's because we were thinking of big steps—travel to faraway places for extended periods of time. One day we just took off and traveled to a seaside village about twenty miles from home. We spent the day there and returned refreshed. Small steps, we found, do make a difference.

Why Play?

Why play? "What kind of a question is that?" a friend asked us. "Everyone knows why you play—because it's fun." Well, yes. But fun is only part of it. Remember the old adage "All work and no play makes Jack a dull boy"? It carries a timeless truth—you need a balance between the serious and the playful in your life. The adage just doesn't go far enough. Without play, dullness is not all you will endure. Your body, your emotions, and your relationships will also suffer.

We have found that most couples have the *desire* to play, but many are not aware of their *need* to play. Even though they have the desire, they are often like dull Jack or those busy people we discussed in the last chapter. They have allowed the demands of life to so cram their schedules that they have little or no time for play. So before we discuss the ways you can incorporate more play into your relationship, we want to impress on you the incredible benefits you gain when you do play together.

You Are Made for Play

In the beginning, we are all playful. Our brains appear to be hard-wired with both the capacity and the need for play. In other words, play is part of the nature of humans and, in fact, of most of the animal kingdom. You don't have to teach a puppy or a kitten to play. It comes naturally. And they continue to play even as they grow older. Even after her sprinting and bounding had slowed to a labored trot, our family dog, Licorice, delighted in a romp at the park. After her legs began to fail, her ears still perked up at the mention of the park.

Animals in the wild also play throughout their lives.[1] For example, African elephants have been observed frolicking in the rain—running, flapping their ears and trunks, spraying each other with water, and emitting the particular trumpet sound associated with play. Adult spotted hyenas have been seen playing in a river, splashing, pushing each other under water, and jumping back and forth between the bank and river. And at least since the time of Darwin, observers have recognized that chimpanzees and other great apes emit a sound that is similar to laughter when they are tickled or play with each other.

Animal play, like that of humans, does more than just provide fun. (Although many specialists bristle at the thought of attributing human qualities to animals, we believe that animals have fun when they play.) Some ethologists, in fact, believe that play may be as important as eating and sleeping for a number of species.[2] When animals like wolves and primates play, they are, at the same time, creating and maintaining solidarity within the group. Thus, play occurs between members of a pack of wolves but not with members of other packs. It's as if the play is a way of affirming that "we are members of the same group; we are one."

Play also helps animals learn to respond properly when they confront various kinds of behavior in other animals. When grizzly bears cavort around salmon streams in the summer, for instance, the young bears learn the difference between behaviors that signal a threat and those that indicate playfulness. They come to recognize whether an adult bear is inviting them to a romp or challenging them to battle.

Humans are no less inclined to be playful. If you don't think of yourself as playful, it isn't because you're just a serious person by nature. It's because your life circumstances have somehow managed to wring you dry, suppressing those play impulses that danced around in you during childhood.

Anyone who has watched a baby develop knows an infant begins to play early in life. Babies start laughing at about three or four months of age and quickly begin engaging in playful games with adults. By the age of six, children know how to joke. Play changes, of course, when the child becomes an adult, as poker replaces peek-a-boo. But the enjoyment continues.

So does your *need* for play. If chimpanzees are deprived of play when they are young, they are likely to grow up to be hostile, withdrawn, and incapable of parenting. Similarly, when human infants are deprived of play, they develop problems adjusting to new situations and getting along with others.[3] And these problems may continue into adulthood.

The dire consequences of play deprivation were dramatized by the horrifying plight of children raised in Romanian orphanages during the 1990s. These children were seriously deprived of both love and play. They lay in their beds without anyone to give them attention or anything to provide stimulation. Not surprisingly, most have evidenced depression and antisocial behavior in subsequent years. Even the efforts of adoptive parents to provide a loving, stable home have generally failed to change their emotional responses. The absence of caring and playful adults when they were infants may have crippled them emotionally for the rest of their lives.

The need for play is acute among the young and continues to be crucial as we age. Adults who get mired in excessive demands and have no time for play are likely to be unhappy, unfulfilled, unappealing, and un-everything else that really matters to their quality of life. King Solomon observed nearly three thousand years ago, "A cheerful heart is a good medicine, but a downcast spirit dries up the bones" (Proverbs 17:22, rsv). And from their own experience, people have repeatedly told us that play is a good medicine, both for them personally and for their relationships:

> "Jay can always make me laugh. He knows that I typically take myself too seriously, and his silliness provides the perfect antidote."
>
> —*A twenty-nine-year-old saleswoman*

> "When we play, I feel free from the stresses of my job and really bonded with my husband."
>
> —*A forty-three-year-old teacher*

> "What we think of as play has changed over the years, but one thing hasn't changed—the way that play brightens our days together."
>
> —*A fifty-five-year-old businessman*

The point is, if you resist the urge to play, you go against your nature. And when you go against your nature, you harm yourself and expose your relationship to serious damage.

Play Nourishes

We can't say it too often: you are, by nature, a playful creature, and play is, by nature, a nourishing activity. Play nourishes you both physically and emotionally. This is true even when you are engaging in solitary play—fishing, painting a picture, jogging, or immersing yourself in a computer game. Yes, we know that some people get obsessed with such activities and actually strain their bodies and emotions. But then it's no longer play; it's an addiction. As long as it's play, it nourishes you.

You need some time for solitary play, a time when you attend to your own needs. And personal play is good for you as a couple. The healthier you are physically and emotionally, the better your mood.

The better your mood, the easier it is for you to be an enjoyable and exciting partner.

Of course, you need time for couple play as well. In addition to nourishing you physically and emotionally, couple play directly and intensely adds zest to your relationship. It strengthens your bonds with each other. And, as we'll discuss in the next section, it gives you an important tool for coping with various challenges and problems.

Play Fosters Your Physical Well-Being

Catherine, an in-house lawyer with a large brokerage firm, had an experience of play with her husband that transformed her from feeling "really frazzled from too much work" to feeling like "a new woman":

> "The problem was, I never got away from my work. When I was at home, I was thinking about it. Or someone would call. Or I'd check my E-mail and find a dozen messages from the firm. One Friday night when I came home bone-weary, I found a surprise waiting for me. Mike had decided that even though we couldn't take a vacation, I needed time off from work. He had turned the telephone ringer off so we couldn't hear it. He unplugged the computer. He told me to go take a slow bath while he got dinner ready. Actually, he had ordered in Chinese. He gave me our portable CD player with the headphones so I could listen to music rather than think about work while I bathed."

After dinner, Mike cleaned up the dishes, lit some candles, and began the second phase of his plan:

"Take off your shoes," he told Catherine.

"What?"

"Take off your shoes."

"Why?"

"Just take them off."

He had bought a book on foot massage and was ready to try it out on her. Because it was the first time, there was more fumbling and tickling than actual massage. But Catherine loved it and even added that it really turned her on.

In the morning, Mike told Catherine to dress casually for a special treat. He had arranged for both of them to get a professional full-body massage that Catherine said left her feeling "loose as a goose." Afterward they had lunch and wandered around some nearby shops. In the evening, they returned to something they had not done since the early days of their relationship—a rousing game of Scrabble. By Sunday morning, Catherine felt like a new woman. When she returned to work on Monday, she was energetic and even eager for the challenges of the day.

When you play together, you give your bodies a respite from the tensions and stresses of everyday living. You can probably reach into your own memory and pull out a number of illustrations about the renewing effects of play on your own body. Here is the way a therapist described one of his experiences:

> "My work can be draining. At times it saps me both emotionally and physically. A few weeks ago my body felt like a rubber band that was stretched to the breaking point. My wife told me I even *looked* stiff. We had planned to spend the evening cleaning the apartment. Instead, we called some friends, went out for dinner, and laughed at each other's funny stories. By bedtime, my rubber-band body had relaxed. By the next morning, I was ready to return to work."

An evening of laughter and fun was exactly what our friend needed. Indeed, recent research has underscored the healing power of laughter.[4] Laughter boosts your immune system and enhances the well-being of your body in a number of ways, namely, by

- increasing the number of antibodies in your system
- lowering serum cortisol levels (serum cortisol is released by the adrenal gland when you are stressed)
- releasing endorphins (your body's natural painkiller)
- exercising the lungs (which can actually help people with emphysema)
- exercising stomach and chest muscles
- increasing the amount of oxygen in your blood

The composer who wrote the old song "You're My Everything" probably didn't have antibodies, endorphins, and exercise in mind as part of the "everything." It doesn't strike a romantic note to say to your partner, "You're like an endorphin to me." Nevertheless, when you play together, you are giving both yourself and your partner a marvelous dose of tonic. And then, as Catherine and the therapist found, there's the bonus: play time brings new zest to your relationship.

Play Contributes to Emotional Well-Being

Emotional well-being. It has a nice sound. To us, it means more than being free of some kind of mental disorder. We think of emotional well-being as what you have when:

- You experience, overall, more positive than negative emotions.
- You feel sufficiently stable emotionally to deal with the demands and challenges of life.
- You feel good about yourself.
- You are generally optimistic about your future.

When you play together, you help both yourself and your partner to achieve this state. There are a number of reasons why this is so.

Play Helps You Cope with Stress Too much stress is emotionally and physically destructive. Stress is a subtle demon that can drive you into moodiness, depression, anger, and feelings of inadequacy. If you face ongoing stress or a period of intense stress, you need times of respite in order to retain emotional balance. Play gives you a break—a time for the mind to renew and recharge itself.

When Catherine came to the end of her playful weekend, more than her body was reenergized:

> "The cobwebs had been swept from my mind and, as Mike reminded me, the burr was out of my pants. I was so worn down that I had gotten really irritable with my colleagues, as well as with Mike. I was short-tempered, tense, and depressed. Looking back on it, I'm surprised that Mike could put up with me. At any rate, the weekend was like a cleansing of my whole being. All the physical and mental dirt was washed away."

Play Liberates You from Routine Too much routine is also deadly to the human spirit. People who work at repetitive jobs or who are in relationships crushed by dull predictability find themselves longing for something new and stimulating. Undoubtedly, we all need a measure of stability, but we also need a certain amount of excitement and novelty.

A husband who asked his wife about her diminishing interest in sex got the unsettling response, "Our sex life is boring." Yes, even sex can be boring if it becomes routine and devoid of playfulness. Together this couple worked on developing a more playful sex life (a topic we'll explore in Chapter 7), ending both his frustration and her feelings of boredom. Both experienced a new vitality in their marriage generally and in their sex life in particular.

Play Recaptures Some of the Freedom and Spontaneity of Childhood Reflect for a moment on the following adjectives: *inhib-*

ited, prim, repressed, and *solemn.* These adjectives, sadly, describe all
too accurately some adults we know. But if we described a child in
the same terms, we would be more than sad—we would be seriously
concerned. We expect children to be spontaneous, silly, and fun-
loving. And we worry if they are not.

Although we don't advocate that you become childish or cast off
every restraint, we do believe that you still need a measure of freedom and spontaneity. Your spirit soars when you occasionally go with
the urges of the moment and feel free of social restraints. This need
for freedom and spontaneity can be met in play.

For example, Millie is a movie buff and has a knack for imitat-
ing her favorite stars. She's shy about exhibiting her talent, except
with her fiancé Tom. Often, Tom spontaneously gets into the act,
and they play out a scene from one of their favorite movies. Millie
says they usually end up collapsing in laughter.

Play Builds Emotional Capital You enhance your emotional well-
being when you are absorbed in play. What is absorbing, of course,
varies from one couple to another. For you and your partner, it may
be climbing mountains or playing Monopoly or hosting a wine-
tasting party or watching movies until your vision is blurred. Whatever your fascination, go for it! These experiences add emotional
capital to your lives.

You can understand what we mean by *emotional capital* if you
compare it with *emotional baggage.* Psychologists use the term *emotional baggage* to describe the lingering effects of past negative experiences that detract from your present well-being. *Emotional capital*
refers to the continuing effects of past positive experiences that
strengthen your well-being and provide emotional reserves to deal
with the demands and challenges of life. Play is one of those positive
experiences that build emotional capital.

Play Provides an Opportunity to Be Creative We believe that
every person has the potential to be creative and needs to express

creativity. When you do something creative, you feel better about yourself. You feel more fulfilled, more alive.

Some people are fortunate enough to have work that fosters creativity. Everyone, however, can be creative through play because virtually all play has creative possibilities. For example, if you attend the theater together, you can exercise your creativity by discussing insights you gained from the performance or by inventing new lines or scenes you'd like to add to the play. If you go dancing, invent a new dance step. If you read mysteries, try plotting a thriller together. When you plan a vacation, find something different to do, something you've not done together before (have you ever thought about volunteering at an archaeological dig or bicycling across France?). Each time you get creative in your couple play you add to your emotional capital.

Play Enlarges Your Self-Understanding Everything you do—the way you react to challenges, the manner in which you relate to people, and the interests you pursue—gives you insights about the kind of person you are. Play adds to this self-understanding. It taps into facets of yourself that do not appear in other kinds of activities. It helps you to see the breadth and richness of your personality.

Millie and Tom learned something about themselves—something they liked—by letting themselves go and acting out movie scenes:

> "A lot of people think we're pretty serious. And in a way we are. We're both getting started in our careers. That's serious! Before I met Tom, I had my nose to the grindstone. With him, I discovered how free and just plain silly I can be. It makes us feel like kids again. And it makes us feel like we've got a really special relationship, because we do things with each other we won't do with anyone else."

Play Strengthens the Sense of *We*

As Tom and Millie illustrate, couple play makes your relationship unique. You are building your own special world. You are, as we like to put it, strengthening your sense of *we*. Couples with meaningful and lasting relationships move from thinking in terms of *I*, *me*, and *you* to *we* and *us*. And play, including the use of humor, is one of the central factors in enhancing a sense of *we*. A study of young married couples found that the most frequent function of humor was to make the couple feel more cohesive.[5]

In our study of long-term marriage, we were surprised to learn how important a sense of humor was to the three hundred couples we interviewed. Nothing we had read in the professional literature suggested that humor was among the most important factors in a lasting relationship. But nearly three-fourths of our couples said that they laugh together at least daily and that it was an important ingredient in the success of their marriages.

Play, then, adds glue to your relationship. The more you play together, the stronger your bond.[6] We have yet to meet a couple who did not find play to be a bonding and enriching element in their relationship. As a young woman put it:

> "When Ben and I laugh and play together, I just forget about everything else—all my worries and concerns and responsibilities. I feel like holding him close and never letting go. I also know our play times have helped us through the tough times in our relationship. Like when we seem to disagree about everything and our future together seems hopeless. But then I remember the fun times and the intimate moments and I know that we can work through the disagreements."

The good news is that the process tends to be self-perpetuating: the more you play, the stronger the bond; and the stronger the bond, the freer you feel to play.

Why is it that play makes you feel close to one another? What is it about play that develops bonds of unity? Paradoxically, one reason is that play allows each of you to retain your individuality. A cohesive team, for instance, consists of individuals who each make a unique contribution to the group. For couples, we like to use the analogy of two pieces of a jigsaw puzzle that fit together beautifully and are necessary for each other, but are still recognizable as individual pieces.

That's what happens in play. Each partner contributes something unique to the play. Millie needs Tom, either as her audience or as a fellow actor, when she plays a part. And Tom needs Millie, for he wouldn't have that play experience if it weren't for her. They are two individuals, each making their own unique contribution and building a sense of *we* in the process.

Play also helps couples become more cohesive because it is a way of saying you have a very special relationship. As Tom and Millie found, it is only with those close to you that you are free to be spontaneous, childlike, and downright silly. When you play with someone, you are saying, "I like you and enjoy being with you." You are also saying, "I trust you enough to let go of my inhibitions and be silly with you."

How uninhibited? How silly? We suggest that you apply the blush test. We believe that every well-bonded couple has done things together in the course of play that they would not want to share with anyone else. They would blush if forced to reveal their play secrets. If you haven't done things together that you keep locked up between you, you have a play deprivation and fail the blush test. But if you blush at the thought of sharing, you know what it means to say that play develops the sense of *we* and you pass the test.

Play Irons Out the Wrinkles

Life is full of wrinkles. Clothes wrinkle. People wrinkle. Relationships wrinkle—the result of accumulated problems and annoyances. We recommend that you try play when you need something to unwrinkle your relationship.

Draw on Play for Problem Solving

You will always face problems of one sort or another—the insufferable coworker, the interfering relative, the tormenting home appliance. Even if it's a problem in which only one of you is directly involved, it will most likely affect you both. For example, Karen is a medical biologist who loves her work but detests her supervisor. The supervisor's arbitrary and tyrannical way of running his department caused Karen to go home many days feeling irritable and exhausted. Although the problem was hers, it put deep wrinkles into her marriage. She reached the point where she had to deal with the situation before her health was impaired and her marriage was damaged.

When you're in a relationship with someone there is no such thing as *my* problem; it always becomes *our* problem to some degree. Karen couldn't simply turn off her irritability and upgrade her exhaustion to energy when she walked in the door. She found herself being short-tempered with her husband Clark and preferring to be alone. Clearly, Karen's work problem had also become a problem for their marriage.

Karen and Clark had some basic skills in problem solving. They knew the value of brainstorming and evaluating creative alternatives and then agreeing on a course of action. We encouraged them to add another tool to their repertoire: play. Play increases your problem-solving ability by providing needed emotional and physical capital to tackle the problem in a creative and energetic way. If you're low on energy and motivation, a difficult problem will seem nearly impossible to resolve. Clark learned this the hard way. He decided one evening that he was going to help Karen tackle her problem and reduce the tension at work. But the timing was off. Karen had just arrived home from work—tired, frustrated, and angry. Rather than finding a solution, the discussion only increased her anger and frustration.

Clark realized that his effort had made the situation worse. He suggested that they institute a new rule: Talk about work was off limits until after they had time to unwind and relax. Karen began "decompressing" by running with the dog after she got in from work while Clark fixed dinner. By the time they had finished dinner, they were both in a better frame of mind to take on the problems of the day, including ways to help Karen deal with her boss and ways to keep her work problems from infecting their marriage.

Play has some direct uses in problem solving as well. You can draw on it *as needed* while you're working on a problem. We underscore "as needed" because serious problems do require serious work. At the same time, a dose of playfulness is useful in a number of ways.

Playfulness Can Keep Tension and Frustration Under Control
Tension and frustration can build to the point where they quash creative action. Think a bit about Karen's problem with her supervisor. What are her options? After considering the obvious ones—getting a different job or accepting her supervisor's obnoxious behavior as unchangeable and shrugging it off—what's left? Rather than stewing in frustration or giving up, a playful response such as joking about "hiring someone to knock him off" can relieve tension and start the creative juices flowing again.

Playfulness Can Be Used to Get a Sensitive Point Across Clark knew that part of Karen's problem was her tendency to say nothing when her supervisor was being harsh and unfair. She would just seethe quietly and pay the price in a tension headache or an upset stomach. How could he point this out to her? One way was to confront her in an accusatory tone: "Your problem is that you knuckle under to the jerk and let him run all over you." Clark actually tried this approach, and the results were counterproductive. Karen got very defensive and listed the reasons why she couldn't speak up.

Clark made the same point more effectively when he injected a little playfulness into his observation: "I wonder how the tyrant would react if you just said to him one day, 'Hey, bonehead, that's not true and you know it.'" Putting the issue into playful terms helped Karen acknowledge that she didn't stand up for herself and that she needed to find ways to assert herself without jeopardizing her job.

Play Can Pull You Back into Reality It almost sounds like a contradiction. Isn't play an escape? Yes, but moments of irrationality hit us all. At such times, logic and reason are useless. So if at some point you or your partner slips into irrationality, try a dash of play instead. Psychiatrist William Betcher wrote about a wife of ten years who said that her husband had gotten "totally irrational only a few times."[7] One time was when the Internal Revenue Service kept billing them for payments that had already been made. Her husband ranted and raved obsessively about the matter, wearing her down. One night when he was angrily complaining, she acted on an impulse and said, "You're right. I have to take my panties off to this." She then reached under her dress and ripped her panties off. Her action startled her husband into silence. His rage dissipated. And later that evening they had sex, which they hadn't had for several days because of his bad mood. Where none of her efforts at reasonableness made any difference, the playful act brought matters back into perspective for her husband.

Playfulness Can Be an Effective Technique for Coping with a Problem Could a playful response work with Karen's supervisor? We made the suggestion carefully because not everyone responds well to a playful attempt. It was a decision that Karen had to make. She decided it might work and was worth the risk. She had an opportunity when her supervisor upbraided her for omitting some information from a report. He was being unfair; he had given her a short deadline, which limited her data search. She didn't feel she could tell him that he was partly responsible. That would only make him angrier and more reproachful. So instead, she smiled slightly and said, "Am I really such a screw-up? You make me feel like Lucy

Ricardo and Ethel Mertz wrapped up into one." He looked blankly at her for a moment, then said in a milder tone, "I'm not saying you're a screw-up. I'm just saying that this report isn't complete enough." Karen assured him that she would be more careful in the future as long as she had sufficient time. Her playful response probably won't end his unfair criticisms. But she feels better for standing up to him and seeing him back down a little. That evening, she went home and greeted Clark in high spirits.

Use Play to Resolve Annoyances

Asked what she had learned since her marriage a year earlier, Barbara said, "I've learned just how many things Paul does that are really annoying." She said this half jokingly, but also half seriously. She had learned what we all eventually learn about our partners—they can be fairly irritating creatures at times. And it's these irritations and annoyances that bring relationships "made in heaven" crashing back to earth. What can you do when your relationship is wrinkled by annoyances?

Keep Annoyances in Perspective Whether your relationship is exciting or exhausting depends on how you handle the conflict that grows out of your dissimilarities—your different habits, preferences, and styles. You may want the house always neat, while your partner has no problem with messy surroundings. You may prefer to eat at home at 6 P.M. on the dot, while your partner prefers to eat out whenever the mood strikes. You may be very fashion conscious, while your partner pays little attention to what either of you wears. You each are learning how annoying the other can be.

These annoyances can be nettlesome. In some cases, they can be disastrous. A man told us, in complete seriousness, that he and his wife had divorced because they fought incessantly over where to squeeze the toothpaste tube. She squeezed from the top, and he squeezed from the bottom. While we suspect that something more was going on with this couple, their experience does illustrate the point that annoying differences can be perilous. At the very least, they will likely lead to arguments.

Unfortunately, when annoyances produce conflict, most couples follow their base instincts and adopt an attack/defend mode: "You're wrong and I'm right." It would be hard to come up with a more destructive way for a couple to argue. It blows the whole matter out of perspective. A better approach is to think of your dissimilarities not as a battle to be won but as a challenge to your creativity. You are challenged to come up with a way to deal with the issue so that it no longer intrudes into your relationship.

To do this, begin with the premise that "*we* face a challenge" rather than "*you* are annoying." Even if the conflict is about an outrageously annoying behavior of your partner, you are likely to get sucked into an unproductive argument if you start out with "*you* are annoying." The situation involves not only your partner's behavior, but your reaction to it. And because the behavior threatens your intimacy, you need to tackle it as a team.

Incidentally, it will help you to keep the focus on "*we* face a challenge" if you remind yourself that you are an annoyer as well as an annoyee. Your partner's behavior may be the focus of conflict this time, but sooner or later it will be something you have done or not done that results in the conflict.

Use Play as You Creatively Resolve the Annoyance Play is useful in a number of ways to creatively resolve annoyances. For one thing, you can use a playful response to break the tension or make a sensitive point. Consider Mark and Leslie's situation. Mark is an extremely organized person and has the perfect system for doing everything; Leslie takes a more casual approach to life. She discovered how organized Mark is the first time she did the laundry after they were married. Laundry was easy for Leslie—she threw the clothes in the machine, tossed in a little detergent, and turned the thing on. "No big deal," she told us. "But it was to Mark. He was horrified when he found out that a pair of my red undies had faded on his white T-shirt." When the situation threatened to get ugly, Leslie was able to lighten the moment by telling him that he would look sexy in pink. "That took the steam out of his anger and made him laugh," Leslie reported. "The crisis was over for the time being."

You can also use play to deal more reasonably with an issue. We remember our very first argument as a married couple. We don't remember what we argued about. We do remember what happened. It was bedtime. We were at an impasse in our discussion. Bob had grown up in a home where people sulked. So he simply announced that he was going to sleep and turned off the light—a classic method of avoidance. In the darkness, Jeanette began to hum loudly. "What in the world are you doing?" Bob asked her. "I don't think we should go to sleep until we get this settled," she said. The lights came back on. We worked through the disagreement. Had Jeanette tried to harangue him or shame him into continuing the discussion, the impasse would have continued. Her playful action got results.

Use Play for Crabgrass Problems In our experience, no matter what you do, you never get rid of crabgrass permanently. We have had seasons of freedom, but sooner or later a bit of the pesky green reappears and we have to take action again.

Similarly, couples often deal effectively with an annoying problem only to find the matter periodically resurfacing. We call these the crabgrass problems of relationships. For example, if Leslie thought she had altered Mark's organized approach to life by making light of her casual handling of the laundry, she was mistaken. When it was time to do the laundry the next time, Mark instructed her about the perfect system—one that he had inherited from his mother and one that totally mystified her. At first she thought to herself, *How cute and quaint!* But before long, Mark's "perfect system" about laundry extended to other things. His insistence that he knew the perfect way to do everything began to infuriate and intimidate her. As she put it, "He started to drive me bonkers."

Leslie and Mark's dissimilar styles eventually brought their relationship to the breaking point. Their love, commitment, and willingness to change, plus the insights of a skilled therapist, saved their marriage. But not without the added help of their lively senses of humor. "Sometimes all we can do is laugh at how very different we are," Mark said. "Leslie is great—she has a way of poking fun at my obsessive ways in a loving and gentle manner that makes me want to change rather than go on the defensive. And, of course, we have discovered that the love we share is far greater than any of our differences."

So do not—we repeat, *do not*—expect flawless solutions. Even if you both have agreed on a course of action that resolves the issue, there may be an occasional relapse. So what do you do when your partner lapses back into that annoying behavior? Don't give up in despair. Don't assume that he or she is hopeless. And don't nag. Instead, try a little playfulness.

Doris and Kenneth have been dating for a year. They are deeply committed to each other. Yet each of them has traits that annoy the other. Kenneth tends to be like his father, John, who takes his mate for granted and never expresses appreciation for anything she does. And Doris tends to be like her mother, Emily, who nags her husband relentlessly.

Doris and Kenneth realized that they were modeling themselves after their parents, agreed that each of them could change, and worked hard to do so. But there have been lapses. Instead of reacting angrily to the lapses (for example, "Stop acting like your nagging mother" or "Stop behaving like your insensitive father"), they have learned to remind each other playfully of their commitment to alter the annoying patterns. They call each other by the name of the offending parent. If Doris starts nagging Kenneth about something he promised to do, he will say, "OK, Emily, I'll do it." If Kenneth takes Doris for granted, she counters, "Well, John, how did you like that meal I cooked for you?" It works for them.

Play for Keeps

Playing together is a little like selling insurance. There's the thrill of the initial sale. There's also the subsequent commissions that can go on for decades. In like manner, when you play together, you not only get the immediate benefits of the experience but you can also recapture those benefits for years afterward as you recall the experience.

We recommend that you get into the habit of collecting your commissions on old play experiences: "Remember when we . . . ?" Enjoy them again and again.

For this exercise, then, each of you recalls a memorable play experience that you shared. Discuss the following questions: What was it that made this experience so unforgettable for you? Did your partner react to this experience in the same way? Why or why not? Does this experience reveal any differences in your approach to play? What were the benefits of these play experiences for you personally as well as for your relationship?

Understanding Yourself and Your Playful Other

How well do you understand the play preferences and needs of both yourself and your partner (the person we like to call your "playful other")? Maybe not as well as you think you do. Let's try a little experiment. Read the following list of three kinds of couple play and rank them in order of appeal, from the most (1) to the least (3). Then have your partner do the same.

- You spend a week at a Colorado dude ranch. You ride horses, hike, have cookouts, and gather around the campfire every evening.
- You spend a week in New York City, attending a Broadway play each night. In addition to the plays, you enjoy whatever other cultural attractions and fine restaurants you like in the city.
- You take a week off from work to relax at home. You turn off the phone, sleep in, watch TV, read, putter in the garden, and do whatever else suits your fancy.

How did you rank these play experiences? The first is basically an outdoors experience. The second is a cultural affair. And the third is home-centered play. Which type of experience do you prefer? What about your partner? Did you guess correctly how your partner would rank them? To what extent did the two of you agree on your rankings?

Play comes in many varieties. So it's important that you understand both your own and your partner's preferences in order to develop a healthy play life together. A first step is to look at how different or alike you are in those preferences.

Do Opposites Attract?

No doubt, you've heard the old saying "Opposites attract." You may even know couples who seem to have more differences than things in common. Does this mean that people are more likely to be attracted to someone whose play preferences are different from theirs? Does it mean, as one young woman put it, that "we can each do our own thing for play because we just don't like the same things"? The short answer is no. Let's look more closely at the long answer.

Likes Attract

There is a large body of research that indicates that the more you are like someone, the more attracted you are to him or her.[1] In fact, when people are looking for an intimate relationship and meet someone they consider an "opposite," they usually manage to communicate to that person, "I'm not available." This really means, "I'm not available to *you*."

Think about it. You are more likely to be attracted to individuals who are similar to you for several reasons:

- You are more at ease and more confident with those who share your values, lifestyle, and preferences.

- They share your values and attitudes and thus build your self-esteem. In effect, they say, "The way you are is good because I'm that way, too."
- It is easier to share your thoughts and feelings, which is crucial to building intimacy, with those who are like you.

On the other hand, consider a couple of examples of what happens when two people who are opposites try to forge a lasting and meaningful relationship. The first concerns a professional psychologist—a man who should have known better. He announced to us one day that he had gotten married. We were startled because we didn't even know he was serious about anyone. "Who is this mystery woman?" we asked. And the more he talked about her, the greater the mystery. Two people never seemed more dissimilar. Finally, we had to ask, "Just what do the two of you have in common?" Somewhat sheepishly he said, "We have great sex."

Driven by libido into what they thought would be an ecstatic marriage where sex conquered all, they struggled for a few months to establish a life together. But they didn't make it—not even to their first anniversary.

The second couple stayed together for a number of years. In some ways, they were similar to each other. They grew up in the same town and in similar kinds of families. They went to the same high school. They had two small children they both loved. Yet by the time they came to us for help, they were mired in misery.

As we explored their difficulties, it became clear how little they had in common. They disagreed on the best way to raise children. They quarreled about money. They were not compatible sexually. And their interests were strikingly different. He loved to play chess, read, watch the stock market, and spend quiet evenings at home. She loved to dance, go to the movies, party, and travel. The obvious question was, "Why did you get married in the first place?"

Actually, there were two reasons for asking the question. First, we wondered why two people so dissimilar in so many ways would be attracted to each other. And second, troubled relationships can often be helped by going back and recapturing some of the things that brought the couple together in the first place. In their case, however, the answer to the question only added to the bleakness of the situation. The husband summed it up this way:

> "We grew up in the same small town. We started dating in high school. We were never head over heels in love with each other, but there just weren't that many people to date. Pretty soon our family and friends began assuming that we were going to get married. Soon they acted as if it were a done deal. So we did it."

Once out of their small town, they were forced to face up to the reality of their relationship. Despite our efforts to find some basis for keeping them together, they decided to end the marriage.

So do opposites attract? Well, they might. But we're not optimistic about the long-term results. You and your partner may be alike in many ways, but you need to remember that you will always have differences. What's the basis for these differences, and how important are they?

How Alike Are Men and Women in Play?

The popularity of the notion that "men are from Mars and women are from Venus" might lead you to think that all heterosexual couples are a union of aliens. It is true that there are some important differences between males and females, but we don't think you are living with an alien. So how many of these differences are due to gender, and how many to diverse preferences? First, let's look at differences based on gender.

Yes, There Are Gender Differences, But . . .

Gender does account for some of our differences. For example, a number of differences exist between men's and women's sense of humor:[2]

- With verbal humor, men are more likely to be the initiators and women are more likely to be the audience.
- Jokes and funny stories are more often the cause of men's laughter than of women's.
- Women are somewhat more likely than men to laugh at the antics of people and animals.
- Overall, women laugh more than men, but men elicit more laughter than women do.
- At the same time, no differences exist in the extent to which men and women enjoy puns or television comedies.

Notice something important about the differences we listed. "More likely," "more often," and "somewhat more" mean that we are talking about tendencies that reflect relatively small differences. The differences do not apply to many couples. Or sometimes they are even reversed. For example, we know couples where the woman is the initiator and the man is the audience in verbal humor.

In other words, whatever the reasons for the gender differences in humor, they are not rooted in our biological makeup. The same is true of other kinds of play. Women and men enjoy sports. Men and women enjoy cooking. Thankfully, the old stereotypes about which activities are appropriate for men and for women are becoming a part of the storehouse of cultural myths.

In short, whatever differences in play preferences exist between you and your partner may not be attributable to gender differences. Rather, they may reflect the fact that you are two unique individuals.

Yes, There Are Individual Differences, But . . .

Every individual is unique. No one else in all the world is exactly like you. So even if you are linked up with someone who is very much like you, the two of you also will have differences. Our own marriage is a union of two people who are very similar. We have the same social and cultural background. We both grew up in St. Louis. We attended the same high school (though not during the same years). We earned our Ph.D.s from the same university. We are both teachers as well as writers. We share the same faith and political orientation. We have few differences in our values and attitudes about life.

At the same time, we do have differences, and nowhere are these more evident than in our play preferences. For a start, Jeanette loves gardening, aerobic exercise, and gourmet cooking; Bob, on the other hand, loves football, fishing, and computer games.

Every couple could draw up a similar list of play activities that only one of them enjoys. However, every couple we know with a to-die-for relationship can draw up an even longer list of play activities that they enjoy together. Some individual differences in play preferences are inevitable. In fact, they're good, because you need some time for personal play as well as time for couple play.

Take Debbie and Tim, for instance. After a rocky start, they have learned how to make their play differences work for them. According to Debbie, they have always enjoyed many of the same activities—especially swimming, dancing, and going to the movies. But after they married, Debbie says they discovered a troublesome difference:

> "Reading has always been one of my favorite pastimes. It's really a passion I've had ever since I was a little girl. But Tim is a sports freak. He likes to play and he likes to watch. And he'll watch anything from baseball to those big ugly trucks racing around in the mud.
>
> "We didn't realize how much each of those activities meant to us until we got married and were together every day. For a while, we

tried to accommodate both of our loves. We'd cuddle together on the couch, and Tim would watch a sports program while I read. That didn't work. I couldn't concentrate because of the noise.

"It seemed to me that the sports channel was on every waking moment we were at home. I complained about the sound. I was particularly incensed by the inane commentary—at least, that's how I viewed it—of the sportscasters. And my attitude about it began to wear on Tim.

"Finally, one night I knew we had to try something else. I told Tim I was going into the bedroom, then I shut the bedroom door and read. He said it sounded like we were already an old married couple who went their separate ways. That bothered me. I didn't want to start a pattern of doing things separately. But we decided to give it a try. And it's worked for us. When he watches his programs, I read in the bedroom. But we limit ourselves to an hour or two at most."

Their individual play time hasn't detracted from their couple play time, nor from their relationship. "In fact," Debbie notes, "it makes our time together even more enjoyable because we've each had at least a little time to pursue one of the things we really enjoy."

If, like Debbie and Tim, you want to understand your own and your partner's play preferences and make your similarities and differences work for you, you'll find the following *play profile* useful. As you take it, you may discover something about yourself and your partner.

Building a Play Profile

Work separately as you construct your play profiles so that you don't influence each other's responses. It's important that you respond according to your personal likes and dislikes and without regard to how you think your partner feels about them.

My Play Profile

First, number from 1 to 30 along the margin of a sheet of paper. These numbers represent the thirty activities in the play profile. Then score each of the activities, using the following scale to indicate how much you like or dislike it:

> 1—Strongly dislike
>
> 2—Dislike
>
> 3—Neither like nor dislike
>
> 4—Like
>
> 5—Strongly like

If you've never tried a particular activity, you may score it as a 3 or you may score it in accord with how much you think you might like or dislike it.

1. Attending parties
2. Dining out with other couples
3. Involvement in political or social action groups
4. Hosting parties
5. Participating in a book group or gourmet cooking club
6. Going to museums
7. Attending concerts
8. Going to the movies
9. Traveling
10. Doing arts and crafts
11. Telling jokes or funny stories
12. Listening to jokes or funny stories
13. Acting silly
14. Watching comedies on television
15. Finding humor in day-to-day events
16. Playing board games
17. Working jigsaw puzzles
18. Playing computer games
19. Playing cards

20. Playing charades
21. Hiking
22. Participating in sports
23. Watching sporting events
24. Doing aerobic workouts
25. Camping
26. Taking a shower with your partner
27. Flirting with your partner
28. Hugging and holding hands with your partner
29. Writing love letters to your partner
30. Having sex with your partner

What Is Your Play Profile?

When you have finished scoring each activity, you are ready to complete your play profile. The thirty activities represent six different types of play. The first five activities represent *social play*, followed by *cultural play* (6 through 10), *humor* (11 through 15), *games* (16 through 20), *physical play* (21 through 25), and *love play* (26 through 30). Add the numbers you put down for each group of five activities to get your score for each type (it will range from 5 to 25). Record your answers on your sheet. Your scores for the various categories represent the extent to which you like or dislike the differing types of play.

For example, an individual's scores might look like this:

1. Social play—12
2. Cultural play—15
3. Humor—20
4. Games—8
5. Physical play—22
6. Love play—22

Clearly, the person with these scores has minimal interest in games, some interest in social and cultural play, and a strong desire for humor, physical play, and love play.

How Do You and Your Partner Compare?

If your rankings are similar, you have cause to celebrate. It's easier to increase the amount of couple play if you share likes and dislikes. But what if the rankings differ? They probably will to some extent. It will just take a little more effort to find the kinds of couple play that work for you. For activities that only one of you strongly likes, you may decide, like Debbie and Tim, to use them as individual play. It isn't necessary that your couple play be confined to activities that are your first preference. Neither Debbie nor Tim, for example, would put dancing as one of their top preferences for play. But if her reading and his watching sports bring rewards to them, so does their dancing, as Debbie explained:

> "As I said, I love to read. I like to dance, too, but I wouldn't choose dancing over reading. I have to admit, though, that I feel great after spending a night dancing with Tim. And it's a wow for our love life."

Fortunately, Debbie and Tim are more alike than different in their preferences. What if the two of you differ drastically? Can you still find happiness together? It won't be as easy for you, but we believe the answer is still yes. Keep in mind that we have given only five examples in each play category. There are many more, so that even someone who ranked, say, physical activities at the bottom should be able to find a particular physical activity that he or she enjoys. Thus, if you put physical play at the top of your list and your partner put it last, you need not abandon that category as part of your couple play. Keep exploring until you find something you both enjoy.

If you go through all the examples in this book, including the lengthy list in the last chapter, we believe that you will find many different kinds of play that you both will find appealing. What about the couple we discussed earlier, who had few common interests but who had married because family and friends expected it? We believe even their relationship could have been salvaged. By the time we encountered them, however, they were clearly determined to break up. They may have come to us only to assuage their own consciences and make their families think that they had done their best to work through their differences.

Will and Carla, who also differ dramatically in their play preferences, had a very different outcome. They married at an early age, got involved in their careers, raised a child, and generally, as Will put it, "stumbled along in our relationship until Brad left for college. After the shock of the empty nest began to wear off, we realized that our relationship was fairly bankrupt. For years, Brad had been the focus of our life together. Now we felt almost like two strangers living in the same house. It was a real wake-up call."

But Will and Carla weren't ready to give up. They decided that their relationship needed a transfusion of vitality. Carla told us:

"We knew we had to find ways to reconnect. First, we decided that we would work on communication—the 'big C.' For years, our conversation had mainly focused on Brad or on work. So we agreed to spend time each evening talking about ourselves and our marriage. Believe me, it wasn't easy—but we did it. We began talking about our feelings, our hopes, and our desires. And one thing we discovered as we talked was how little play and fun there had been in our marriage.

"So we decided to tackle the 'big P.' We agreed that one reason that there had been so little play in our relationship was that we had such different interests. Will's idea of a fun time is to spend the afternoon swimming in the pool; mine is to shop for antiques with a group of friends. This gives you a hint at our problem."

It hasn't been easy for Will and Carla as they have worked to bridge their differences and add spice to their relationship. But they have persevered and, as Will notes, have found two activities that they enjoy doing together:

> "We have discovered tennis. Carla never enjoyed sports very much, but she really has taken to tennis. She says she can get rid of all her frustrations by whacking the ball around. And I love sports of all kind, so it didn't take much to make me a tennis addict.
>
> "The other thing we have discovered is a mutual love of bridge. We never played until a friend taught us. Now we've joined a bridge club that meets every week. I am intrigued by the intricacies of the game, and Carla enjoys the verbal play around the table."

Will and Carla report that they are having the "time of their lives" and that their relationship "is the best it's ever been."

Will and Carla's experience shows that even couples with diverse play profiles can find common ground and that many play activities fall into more than one category. Bridge, for example, met both Carla's need for social play and Will's love of games. We once combined culture play and games by undertaking a hunt to collect a full set of the Pulitzer Prize novels. After exhausting local sources, we visited used bookstores when we traveled. It became something of a game to see whether we could track an elusive Pulitzer when we explored a new city and to see who would be the first to spot it.

Your play profiles, then, give you a tool to use in enhancing your couple play. Understanding both your own and your partner's preferences, you are better prepared to know what kind of new activities to explore. A second important tool is your *couple play quotient*. Let's look at it.

Your Couple Play Quotient

If your play profile shows your individual preferences, your *couple play quotient* (CPQ) shows the extent to which you feel each kind of play is adequate or lacking in your relationship.

When each of you has finished, take your individual score for each category and add it to your spouse's, then add the six category scores to get your total. Your CPQ is made up of the total score along with the six category scores. (See the sample below.)

The total in your CPQ could range from 0 (which means you are play starved) to 240 (which should make you wonder whether you added correctly). An ideal total score for your CPQ would be 120, assuming you got that score because you each gave 10 points to each category, indicating that you both are quite satisfied with the amount of each kind of play (in which case, we wish we had known you before completing this book). Note that your total score must always be interpreted in the light of the six separate scores. You could, for example, score 120 if you gave 20 to the first three categories and 0 to the last three while your partner did just the opposite (indicating, we might add, that you have some major issues to work on).

Our Couple Play Quotient

Respond individually to each of the six categories of play (refer to the examples in the play profile to remind yourself of the kinds of play involved in each) using the following scoring scheme:

> 0—We do this much less often than I prefer
>
> 5—We do this sometimes, but less than I prefer
>
> 10—We have an adequate amount—as much as I prefer—of this
>
> 20—We do this more than I prefer

1. Social play ——
2. Cultural play ——
3. Humor ——
4. Games ——
5. Physical play ——
6. Love play ——

Here's a sample set of the scores of a fictitious couple (we call them Sam and Diane) that illustrates how to interpret the results:

Sam

1. Social play—5
2. Cultural play—10
3. Humor—5
4. Games—20
5. Physical play—0
6. Love play—5

Diane

1. Social play—10
2. Cultural play—5
3. Humor—5
4. Games—10
5. Physical play—5
6. Love play—5

Sam and Diane's Couple Play Quotient

1. Social play—15
2. Cultural play—15
3. Humor—10
4. Games—30
5. Physical play—5
6. Love play—10
   Total = 85

Diane and Sam fall short of the ideal of 120. Looking at the individual categories, it's clear that they have no need for more games. Sam thinks they already play too many of them. It's possible that in his play profile the category of games was the only one in which he had little interest. Or it may be that he enjoys games but feels that he and Diane spend too much of their time playing them. It's a matter they need to discuss.

Sam and Diane need to attend to the other categories as well, particularly to those with the lowest scores: physical play, love play, and humor. For example, they may need to trade in Monopoly for more frequent walks in the park or tussles in bed. Or they may need to find other ways to incorporate more play time in their lives.

As you discuss your own couple play quotient, make a mental note of the areas where you need to increase your play. In the next chapter, we are going to look at the dark side of play—at those kinds of "play" that are destructive games rather than relationship-enriching fun. But in subsequent chapters, we'll discuss such things as being spontaneous, exercising creativity, and finding play niches in ordinary time. Keep your play profiles and your CPQ handy (or at least in mind) as you work through these chapters. They'll help you find ways to deal with the deficiencies in your couple play. In addition, we're going to devote entire chapters to both humor and love play—because virtually every couple we know would like to add more of both to their lives.

Before we do this, try another exercise at playing for keeps.

Play for Keeps

Most of the couples we have worked with in marriage enrichment weekends, classes, and support groups are able to construct lofty goals for themselves. They want to be more communicative. They want to handle conflict more effectively. They want to be more sensitive to each other's needs. They want to be more playful. And so on.

Setting goals is not the problem; the challenge is reaching them. This is why we urge couples to get very specific, very concrete, as they think about how to reach their goals. Sometimes it takes a lot of prodding, as illustrated by this exchange between an interviewer (I) and subject (S):

I: "What do you want to accomplish?"
S: "We want a stronger marriage."

I: "How will you achieve that?"

S: "We're going to become more playful."

I: "How will you do that?"

S: "We're going to do more things that are fun."

I: "What exactly are you going to do?"

S: "We're going to increase the amount of love play in our relationship."

I: "And just how are you going to do that?"

And on it goes as we strive to get the couple to be specific and develop a workable plan of action. For this exercise, therefore, we want to show you how to be specific. Look at your play profiles again. Take the top two categories for each of you (which could mean a total of two, three, or four categories, depending on how alike you are in your preferences). Only five activities are listed in each category. Work together to extend the lists. Come up with as many activities as you can in each of your most preferred categories. Once you have your lists, go over the activities and decide which ones you both enjoy or would be willing to try together. Then see how many of them you can put on your calendar, keeping in mind that you haven't been sufficiently specific and concrete until you've actually done them.

Let the Player Beware,
or How Not to Do It

Meg and Ed were making marriage plans when their relationship hit a snag. They each complained that the other had changed: Meg felt that Ed had become excessively possessive, and Ed felt that Meg had lost her sense of humor. Here is Meg's side of the story:

"I feel like Ed has me constantly under surveillance and is always questioning my commitment to him. My job involves many business lunches. A couple of months ago, Ed started grilling me about my lunch companions. If I happened to have lunch with a male colleague, which I often do, his cross-examinations seemed more intense. And it goes beyond business lunches.

"He assumes that every man I know comes on to me. If he calls and I'm not home, he wants me to explain where I've been. If I've been out shopping, he wants to know whether a man or woman waited on me. And if it was a man, he'll ask something stupid like whether the guy's eyes popped out when he saw me. Does he think I go around all day encouraging men to make out with me?"

Here is Ed's side of the story:

"Meg is a beautiful woman. I'm just playing around when I ask her how men react to her. I thought she'd recognize that I am really complimenting her. Sure, I do assume that every man comes on to her. I'd do it myself if I wasn't already with her. But that doesn't mean I don't trust her. I thought she knew that I was just teasing and letting her know in a joking way how attractive she is."

Without going into the details of the situation, suffice it to say that Ed is being controlling without realizing it. Although he really does think he's being playful, his lack of awareness doesn't make the "game" he is playing with Meg any less destructive.

Meg isn't sure what motivates Ed. Is he anxious about their relationship? Is he consumed by jealousy? Does he think she isn't committed to him and their relationship? She doesn't know what is going on. One thing she is certain of: she doesn't think that he's being playful or complimentary when he interrogates her. For their relationship to succeed, Ed has to become aware that he is using playful words (at least that's how he interprets them) in an attempt to control Meg. Then, he has to change his behavior.

Like Ed, many people are not fully aware that they are engaging in destructive play.[1] Sometimes they are spurred by serious emotional needs or problems and may need therapy. More often, however, those who engage in destructive play (and this includes most of us at one time or another) are simply unaware of what they are doing and need to become conscious of their actions. We want you to be alert to the kinds of behaviors involved in destructive play and to consider how to change them.

Recall that in Chapter 1 we gave you the rules of couple play. In essence, what you do is only couple play if it isn't work, if you both enjoy it, and if you feel better about yourselves and your relationship afterward. As you will see, destructive play breaks all three of these rules.

The King of the Hill Game

There is a children's game called "king of the hill." One child stands on the top of a hill (when we played it as kids, the hill was generally a large mound of dirt or slope in the yard) and the rest of the group tries to dislodge him or her. The person who manages to topple the old king becomes the new king of the hill. It is clearly a game in which each participant is trying to be the dominant person in the group.

When couples get involved in a king of the hill game, they are similarly engaged in establishing a pattern of dominance and submission. This is what happened to Frank and Carrie. Both of them are athletic and frequently engage in spontaneous roughhousing. It wasn't at all unusual for Carrie to chase Frank around the house and wrestle him to the floor. However, a couple of seemingly innocent pillow fights sounded an alarm for Carrie:

> "The first time it was really fun. It was Saturday morning and we were making the bed together when Frank threw his pillow at me. I whacked him with my pillow and that started it. We went from pillows to tussling in bed. And then we made love. It was great.
>
> "The next time Frank hit me with a pillow, I thought he wanted the same thing—great sex! But he didn't. He just kept on hitting me with the pillow, and a couple of times he whacked me really hard. I asked him to stop, but he wouldn't until I said 'I give up.'"

This kind of behavior raises concerns about Frank. Has the pillow fight turned into a game of dominance and submission for him? Is it his way of demonstrating his superior strength and his belief that Carrie needs to submit to him? Does he have a need to be the king of the hill in his home?

Frank doesn't see it that way:

"I felt really bad that I hurt Carrie. But she throws a pretty mean pillow herself. And when I'm hit, I just strike back without thinking about how hard I'm swinging the pillow."

Frank and Carrie are both competitive individuals. They had both enjoyed the first pillow fight. However, during the second pillow fight they broke all three rules of couple play: it had become work as Frank struggled to win; Carrie did not enjoy the struggle; and it caused her to question the quality of their relationship.

Clearly, their pillow fights were no longer play. But what were they? To understand better what was going on, we asked Carrie some questions:

"Does Frank dominate you in other ways?"

"I don't think so."

"How about other kinds of play? Does he seem to have a need to be the one who wins?"

"No, not really. He *likes* to win when we play racquetball, but he still enjoys himself when I win. And he always tells me I played a good game."

"How about decision making? Who makes the decisions about finances, purchases, and how you spend your time?"

"We both do."

"What if you disagree? Who has the final say?"

"That doesn't happen much. But when it does, I may win or Frank may win. I really don't think Frank tries to dominate me."

As she assessed her situation, Carrie came to the conclusion that the pillow fighting would have to stop. She didn't believe it was a symptom of a deeper problem in their relationship—of a deep need in Frank to dominate her. Nevertheless, it had ceased to be play. It had become what psychiatrist Lenore Terr calls a game that is "too frightening, too murderously competitive."[2]

Any kind of activity in which one partner is determined to be dominant—to make or keep the other submissive—is more likely to be a destructive game rather than play. The aim of play, after all, is not to dominate but to have fun. There may be momentary satisfaction when you stand alone as king of the hill, but it's only true play when your partner is standing beside you rather than submitting to your superiority.

The Fountain of Youth Game

Every day we are bombarded by ads for potions and lotions and all sorts of amazing procedures that assist us in escaping the ravages of age. These products and services flourish because Americans place such a high value on youth. Those who buy into this notion often turn play into the fountain of youth game. Instead of enjoying play for its own sake, they use it to prove their youthfulness.

For example, Drew, now in his sixties, recalls:

"When I was thirty, I played on a basketball team at our neighborhood gym. We only had five or six players on the team, and all of us were in our thirties. Sometimes we played the whole game without a substitute. The other teams in our league were made up mostly of guys in their late teens and twenties. And to make matters worse, they had more players.

"For me, the games were a chance to exercise and have some fun. Usually we lost, but it didn't matter to me. A couple of the other guys, though, didn't see it that way. They wanted to *win* and *prove* that they could keep up with the younger players on the other teams. Of course, they practically killed themselves in the process. In the long run, all they proved was that they weren't as young or as fast as they used to be. And their frustration and gloom when we lost—which was most of the time—put a damper on our fun."

What happened to Drew also happens with couples when one or both partners use play to prove a point. You can see it in:

- The man who drags his partner on a rigorous hiking trip, not to enjoy nature but to prove that he still has the stamina and strength to do it
- The wife who uses baby talk when her husband is displeased with her, not to ease tension but to show that she's like a sensitive young girl who needs care rather than reproof
- The couple who continue to party until the wee hours of the morning, not because they are having a good time but to prove that they are not getting old and staid

Drew made a wise observation about couple play:

"One of the things I've learned about play is that what you enjoy doing will probably change over the years. When we were first married, Billie and I would do silly things. Like I'd hang a towel around my neck and pretend I was Superman and she was Lois Lane. You can imagine the kind of adventures that led to. We still are silly with each other, but not in the same way. I've traded in my Superman persona for something a bit tamer. I no longer leap off the bed with a towel around my neck, but I have mastered a passable Italian accent and the romantic bottom pinch.

"I think it's important for every couple to keep trying new ways to play. Although our tastes have changed, play is still as important to us now as it was when we were in our twenties. But we don't play the same way."

We heartily agree. Be open to new ways to play as you grow older. This isn't to say that you won't continue some kinds of play for most or all of your life. We've seen couples in their sixties and seventies playing tennis; they've obviously been at the game for many decades. We know couples who have made a lifelong venture of enjoying live theater, museums, and other cultural experiences. The point is, play at something because you enjoy it, not to prove that you're as young as you once were.

The Me Game

In the me game, one of the partners is always the center of attraction and attention. The focus of the game is on the benefits it brings to that person. An extreme case is the person with a narcissistic personality. The narcissist strives to be the special individual who is admired and revered in every situation, including play.

We were at a party where a woman who was an accomplished pianist was asked to perform. She began with a classical number, then switched to popular songs. After a few minutes, her husband took over the show, crooning the tunes with elaborate gestures and dancing around the room boisterously. His wife smiled but soon stopped playing. Other people at the party laughed and applauded the couple, but there was clearly a feeling of unease with the whole performance.

We know the couple fairly well, so we were not surprised by his performance. He typically tries to be the focus of attention. He is a textbook example of a narcissistic personality and is incapable of true play. This means, of course, that he also deprives his wife of couple play. This marriage, not surprisingly, didn't survive.

Anyone can get caught up at times in the me game. It doesn't necessarily mean you are a narcissist. You may, for example, be tempted to resort to the me game when your partner or another couple proposes something that doesn't appeal to you. At such times you may be tempted to insist that everyone do what you want to do, in essence saying, "We're not going to play unless we do it on my terms."

This is an unfortunate response; you'll miss a lot of enjoyable experiences if you're only willing to do those things that have a clear and immediate appeal to you. We have each gone reluctantly to an activity that turned out to be a lot of fun. Of course, there will also be times when your initial reaction is correct and you won't enjoy the experience. You can take consolation in knowing that if your partner had a good time, it was still a worthwhile venture.

The Get Even Game

Children learn early in life how to get even. Countless distressed parents have asked a child, "Why did you hit your brother?" only to hear, "He hit me first." To the child's mind, retaliation is completely justified. Many adults, unfortunately, never outgrow such childish morality. They are oblivious to both the importance and the healing power of forgiveness in relationships.[3]

At its worst, getting even may involve an underlying persistent hostility that one partner has toward the other. But it may also reflect temporary feelings of frustration, anger, or hurt. Thus, a husband confessed to us:

> "I was a ballroom instructor for a few years and had agreed to teach my wife some of the more complex steps. I'm embarrassed to admit it now, but we decided to practice one day after we had argued. I guess she thought everything was settled, but it wasn't. I was still fuming on the inside. So when we were dancing, I deliberately stepped on her toes a couple of times and then acted like it was her fault for not following me properly.
>
> "Needless to say, our dance session that day didn't end well. She didn't accuse me of doing it on purpose, but she knew I was a better dancer than that. It came close to ruining our dancing together. What did I learn from the experience? To work through our disagreements until they're over for both of us rather than pretending everything's OK and then getting even. It seems so much easier to get even than to forgive. But I feel tons better when I forgive instead of trying to get back at her."

This husband was right on target when he talked about forgiveness. To forgive each other is the best way to avoid falling into the get even game. Forgiveness is such a powerful tool in an intimate relationship that we are often amazed at how reluctant some people are to exercise it. Of course, you can always come up with a reason for *not* forgiving. For instance, if your partner has hurt you, you may have a desire to get even, and forgiveness won't permit this. Or you may be afraid of getting hurt again, making yourself vulnerable to the same kind of behavior from your partner. Or your partner may not believe that he or she has done anything wrong; how can you forgive someone who isn't sorry? Or you may have been told to "forgive and forget" and you don't see how you can possibly forget something that was hurtful to you.

We don't accept any of these reasons. As long as you harbor resentment, anger, or hurt toward your partner, you can't engage in couple play. A young husband who was angry at his wife because they hadn't had sex in a couple of weeks (her work schedule had left her exhausted) agreed to have some friends over for dinner one weekend. She thought that a fun evening with friends would be a prelude to romance after the guests left. Unfortunately, he interacted warmly with their guests but responded to everything his wife said in short, cold sentences. In the process, he ruined two opportunities for a fun evening—first with their friends, and later with his wife. He got even, but at the cost of intensifying rather than relieving his frustration.

If you or your partner has trouble forgiving, keep in mind what forgiveness is. It doesn't mean that you are erasing the hurt from your memory. Rather, it means you strive to let go of your hurt, forgo any retaliation, and work with your partner to overcome the damage and restore intimacy. Make sure that you tell your partner exactly why you feel the way you do, that your partner understands your feelings, and that you acknowledge your own contribution to the problem. Always, when facing the need to forgive, remember that there is more than one irritating person in your relationship. You need not only to forgive, but also to be forgiven. In other words, if you keep in mind that you are an irritant as well as irritated, it will be easier for you to practice forgiveness. And when you each learn to practice forgiveness as often as necessary, you'll be prepared for more couple play and for a lot more sizzle in your relationship.

The Mystery Game

After being married for many years, we still discover new things about each other. Neither of us is an open book to the other. There is still a hint of mystery. Though a little mystery is good, too much is another matter. There should be no mystery about your play preferences. You need to be clear about what play means to each of you and understand each other's likes and dislikes.

Dennis and Jean, unfortunately, ignored this advice. Early in their marriage, they bought a motorboat that they cruised on a nearby lake most Saturdays during the summer. Dennis saw it as the perfect way to relax and enjoy time with Jean. He eventually suggested that they buy a cabin nearby so that they could stay at the lake the entire weekend. Jean hated the idea. In fact, by this time, she was tired of spending most Saturdays boating. Yet she didn't tell Dennis how she felt. And, although he sensed that something was amiss, he never confronted Jean.

One weekend they had this exchange:

D: "C'mon, Jean, we're going to be late. You're dragging your feet today."

J: "I'm just tired. We'll get there in plenty of time."

D: "Don't you want to go?"

J: "Of course I do. Don't you?"

D: "We go a lot. It's OK if we don't go today."

The interesting thing about the exchange is that neither of them communicated their true feelings to the other. Jean never told Dennis she would like to go to the lake less often. She pretended to still be enthusiastic, but he knew her well enough to question her true feelings. And Dennis acted as if he would be happy to stay home, though he really longed to be at the lake. Neither was certain about how the other really felt. Rather than exploring their feelings, they just did what they did every Saturday: they took off for the lake. But it wasn't couple play for either of them. Jean wanted to be at home, and Dennis couldn't enjoy himself because he sensed her reluctance.

As Jean and Dennis illustrate, the way to avoid the mystery game is to be open with each other. This isn't always easy. Sometimes, like Dennis and Jean, you may not express your true feelings because you are anxious to please each other. Sometimes you mask your feelings because you don't want to risk a disagreement. And sometimes you may not even be sure of what you really feel.

Rick, who had dated Monica for nearly a year, was a champion at the mystery game, mainly because he was uncertain about his feelings for her. He kept saying things that made her question the extent to which he found her attractive and a possible life partner. Yet when she questioned him, he always insisted that he was only kidding. For example, he would say things like:

- "If you're going to order the most expensive item on the menu, we need to start going Dutch treat."
- "Wow, that outfit must have cost a small fortune."
- "I thought we might go away next weekend. But I don't know. Maybe you need to spend the time with your parents."
- "How much time and effort do you think it would take for you to look like one of those models?"

They finally broke up. She couldn't continue dating him and wondering how he really felt about her. She correctly decided that his "kidding" was not a form of couple play, but an indication of his own uncertainty about where he wanted their relationship to go.

The Resident Comic Game

As we noted in Chapter 2, humor is an important tool for building intimacy. Ironically, it can also be used to avoid intimacy.[4] We have an acquaintance whom we've known for over ten years. But we really don't "know" him. We can never get a straight answer from him or have a serious discussion with him because he treats everything as a joke. To know and feel intimate with a person, you need a balanced diet of both the humorous and the serious.

Humor can be used to avoid disagreements or important decisions. For example, the first thing that attracted Brooke to Kevin was his sense of humor. Kevin was a salesman who came regularly to the offices where Brooke worked as a receptionist. "He cracked me up every time he came in," she told us. They soon started going out and were married within a year of their first date. By their first anniversary, they were struggling. Brooke was angry, unhappy, and uncertain whether their marriage would survive. "Kevin never takes anything seriously," she complained. "If I try to talk to him about important things—like buying a house or having children—all I get are his silly wisecracks."

Kevin used his sense of humor and his seemingly endless stock of jokes to sell both his products and himself to other people. Humor had brought Brooke into his life. He expected it to keep her there. If he kept the funny lines coming, he believed, he would always have a great marriage. And so the more troubled his marriage, the more he tried to laugh the problems away. He treated humor as a magic potion that would keep his marriage healthy. But it didn't work.

Take the time when Brooke wanted to discuss buying a larger house so that they could begin a family. The prospect of a larger mortgage frightened Kevin. He had grown up in a home where the main message about money was, "Never be extravagant. You never know how long you'll have it, so be careful how you spend it."

Instead of explaining his fears to Brooke, Kevin responded with one of his comic routines. "Hey," he said to Brooke, "that reminds me of the joke about this old couple who decided to move. . . ." When she insisted that she didn't want to hear any funny stories, that she wanted to talk about their future, he said, "Don't worry about the future, baby—as long as we're together it's going to be fabulous. Listen, I've got to get ready for my sales meeting tomorrow. We'll talk about it later."

What Kevin didn't recognize was the extent to which his role as resident comic was destroying rather than enhancing the quality of his marriage. He finally agreed to work with Brooke in learning how to carry on serious conversations together. They have hit on a device that reminds him when it's time to be serious. The comic Jimmy Durante used to sign off his radio show by saying goodnight to Mrs. Calabash. When Brooke says, "Goodnight, Mr. Calabash," Kevin knows that he needs to stop with the jokes and talk seriously with her about the matter at hand. Brooke, incidentally, doesn't mind his occasional quip. Even serious discussions can have their humorous moments.

The Mad Tea-Party Game

In Lewis Carroll's delightful story *Alice's Adventures in Wonderland*, Alice attends a "mad tea-party" with the March Hare, the Mad Hatter, and the Dormouse.[5] However, Alice's idea of a party clearly differed from theirs. Eventually, she was offended and stalked off. "I'll never *go there* again," she said as she went her way. "It's the stupidest tea-party I ever was at in all my life!"[6]

In the couples' version of the mad tea-party game, one partner drags the other into play activities without considering the interests, preferences, and dislikes of the other. The offending partner ignores a marriage expert's timely advice (it's about humor but is applicable to play generally): "Of course, it's always important to make sure your humor is tempered by empathy and affection. If your partner displays a staunch unwillingness to joke about a particular topic, pay attention to that message."[7]

When you don't pay attention, you may get caught up in the mad tea-party game. Megan found herself trapped in such a game with her athletic husband. Ray had seemed eager to do the things she enjoyed when they were dating. They ate out, went to movies, took long walks on the beach, and attended concerts. However, he seemed to lose interest in these activities after they were married, and increasingly wanted to participate in activities that held little appeal for her. As she tells it:

> "One of Ray's buddies told him how much fun he and his wife had when they backpacked in wilderness areas, so he decided that this would be a great pastime for us to pursue. I *hated* the idea, but he nagged me until I agreed to give it a try. We spent seven weekends last year in the backcountry. I'll admit we trekked through some beautiful areas and the quiet was amazing. But, as far as I'm concerned, these were not enough to offset the disadvantages—the heavy backpacks, limited rations, creepy crawlers, and no bathrooms. I've decided I'm just not an outdoors girl. My idea of roughing it is to stay in a hotel that doesn't have a coffee machine in the room."

At times, Megan has been very close to joining Alice and leaving the party (her marriage) in a huff. She wonders what kind of life she and Ray will have together if they don't become more compatible in their play.

To avoid the mad tea-party game, we suggest that you begin with each other's play profile and explore your various choices. Be specific about what you each like and dislike. Kent has developed a wonderfully playful relationship with his wife Sally. He told us that it was a learning process and didn't happen overnight. For instance:

> "It took me a while to understand what made her laugh. I've learned that blonde jokes and racial jokes really turn her off. But she cracks up at puns. Through a combination of telling and careful observation, we've helped each other learn the kinds of play that are good for us."

The Teasing Game

Teasing has never been a big part of our couple play. We learned early in our relationship that it can easily and quickly slip into a destructive game. We believe that teasing should come with a warning label: Handle with care! As Kent wisely pointed out to us, teasing can be an effective way to play, but it can also be harmful:

> "Teasing creates intimacy if you do it properly. When you tease, and accept teasing, you're saying to each other, 'You're my playmate.' Because teasing is what kids do. It's one way to play. It's a form of joking. But it can also be a way to harass or mock or needle someone. That's why Sally is so sensitive about blonde jokes. As a blonde, she feels like she has had to struggle to be taken seriously as a mechanical engineer. So I've learned not to tease her about the color of her hair."

Teasing is harmful when it makes someone feel defenseless and uncomfortable. This is especially true when, like Christie, you have grown up in a culture of teasing. Christie is the only daughter in a family of four children. "I can't tell you how many times I was teased by my brothers and father to the point of tears," she said. "They would start teasing and then it would snowball. They just didn't know when to stop."

She says that as she looks back on her childhood, she knows that her father and brothers loved her. But that's not the way she felt then. To this day, she hates to be teased. It generates the same feelings that she had as a child. For example, her husband Bud recently teased her about the bright-colored dress she was wearing to a long-anticipated dinner party. "That's quite an outfit," he said. "You're going to light up the room."

"What's the matter?" she asked anxiously. "Is the dress too bright?"

"Not for the guys," he replied. "They'll all love it."

"But do you think that it looks like I'm trying to get attention?" she responded.

"Hey, what's wrong with trying to get a little attention?" he razzed her a bit.

At that point, it was clear to Bud that Christie was getting very agitated. "I'm only kidding," he said. "It looks great."

But Christie, angry and hurt, went to the bedroom and put on a different dress. Bud thought he was "having fun" with her. He thought she'd enjoy hearing that she looked dazzling. Instead, he was reminded that teasing is not the way to have fun with his wife. Past painful experiences have left Christie with little capacity to appreciate even playful teasing.

Only you and your partner can help each other know the extent to which, if any, you enjoy teasing with each other. Here are some examples of teasing both as a destructive game and as couple play:

Destructive Teasing

- "How's my *big* baby today?" (Said to a wife concerned about her weight)
- "What would you like for dinner, baldy?" (Said to a man concerned about losing his hair)
- "Hey, you stick to sewing and let me take care of the E-mail." (Said to a woman who was struggling to work with a computer)
- "After all, you're no Einstein. Why don't you find a different way to relax?" (Said to a husband who couldn't finish a crossword puzzle)

Teasing as Couple Play

- "I'll bet you can't guess what I bought for you today."
- "My wife is an excellent cook . . . as I recall."

- "My husband says he enjoys puttering in the garden. So he'll probably do it one of these days."
- "You're so big and hot. You may be too much for me to handle." (Said to a husband during sexual foreplay)

Can you see the differences? Teasing is a destructive game when it takes the form of putdowns, veiled threats, criticisms, and efforts to have fun at someone else's expense. Teasing is play, on the other hand, when it includes affirmations, suspense, and poking fun at common foibles. As Kent noted, teasing is one way to affirm that you are playmates. Just be careful not to let it slip into a destructive game.

Play for Keeps

A woman complained to us about her husband's lack of affection: "I want him to hug and hold me more. I need a lot of intimate contact." "Did you tell him this?" we inquired. "No," she admitted, "I want him to *know* and *do* it without my having to ask for it."

As we explained to her, no matter how close, how intimate, you are with someone, you can't expect that person to always know what you need or prefer. Thus, at various points in this chapter, we have stressed the importance of being open and honest with each other about your play preferences in order to avoid slipping into any of the destructive games. So your first task is to review the games and talk frankly with each other about whether you have gotten entangled in any of them. If so, discuss how you can avoid doing so in the future.

Your second task will be more enjoyable. In contrast to, and in rebuke of, the destructive games, select a game that brings you together as equals, involves something you both enjoy, and allows you to wager on the outcome. Your wager could be that the loser will have to take over a task disliked by the winner for a week. One possibility for the game is a kissing contest. You are to kiss until one of you loses by stopping for a breath or by breaking the kiss by laughing. It's the kind of game where even the loser is a winner.

5

A Laugh a Day

What's the secret of a to-die-for relationship? Whenever we pose that question to couples, we get their instant attention. Clearly, people want this kind of relationship. Just as clearly, they hope there's an easy formula that will help them achieve it. But that formula does not exist. Relationships aren't simple matters.

Still, based on our work with couples, we have developed a number of principles that help secure a lively and lasting relationship. One principle is this: *A laugh a day keeps the relationship blahs away.* Yes, it's simple. But it's no simpler than the old adage "An apple a day keeps the doctor away." Both sayings express a truth rather than give a comprehensive formula for success. The "apple a day" principle points out the importance of good nutrition. The "laugh a day" principle underscores the importance of shared fun. As we pointed out in Chapter 2, the great majority of couples who have lasting, happy marriages report that they laugh together every day.

"But," you may object, "you don't know my situation. You don't know the problems I'm facing. There's very little to laugh about in my life right now." That may be true. Then again, we don't know of anyone who doesn't have problems. For example, we know very few people who encountered the kind of laughter-quenching situations endured by those in Nazi concentration camps. The late psychotherapist Viktor Frankl was imprisoned in four different Nazi death camps, including Auschwitz, during World War II. After the war, he wrote that humor is "another of the soul's weapons in the fight for self-preservation."[1] As he pointed out, humor helps people rise above the most dehumanizing situations, even if only for a few moments.

Frankl told how he "practically trained" a fellow prisoner to develop a sense of humor as a survival skill. He got the prisoner to agree that each of them would invent a funny story every day. The story would be based on something that might happen after they were free again. He found that moments of laughter in the camps were not only possible but crucial to survival.

So if you feel you are in a situation that makes laughing together every day an impossibility, we recommend reading Viktor Frankl. Laughter, as he shows, isn't a way to deny or ignore your troubles— it's a tool to help you survive them and to knit your two souls into one in spite of assaults on your well-being. For better and for worse, the "laugh a day" principle applies.

You're convinced. You agree with the principle. "The question is," you say, "how do we implement it?" Here are ten ways to bring more laughter into your relationship:

1. Accept your laughter debt.
2. Keep things in perspective.
3. Create a laughter-friendly environment.
4. Raise your humor awareness level.
5. Be a collector of humor.
6. Relive past times of laughter.
7. Be a producer and consumer of humor.
8. Choose to see the humorous side of things.
9. Try going out of character.
10. Expect it to happen.

Let's examine each of these.

Accept Your Laughter Debt

We view marriage as a commitment between two people to love, honor, cherish, and *entertain* each other until death do them part. If you're not married but in a committed relationship, you have the same obligations. You owe your partner a great deal of laughter. It will take a lifetime to pay off the debt.

Some people object when we say these things. It isn't politically correct in an age of "me-ism," with its focus on self-fulfillment, to assert an obligation to entertain another person. "You're responsible for your own entertainment," we are told. "You have no right to expect your partner to keep you laughing."

In response, we want to make four points. First, you have every right to expect your partner to entertain you, because it's a mutual obligation. You are obligated to entertain as well as to be entertained. We're not talking about an entertainer/audience relationship. We're advocating mutual responsibility and mutual benefit in maintaining a laughter-rich life.

Second, what is the point of your relationship? You didn't commit to one another in order to annoy and make each other miserable. Rather, you joined together because you hoped to make each other happier. So why not accept this as a lifelong task?

Third, we are not suggesting that you constantly keep each other in stitches. The serious and the routine are a part of all our lives. But these need to be punctuated with times of laughter. For instance, make a point of coming up with amusing observations when you are stuck in rush-hour traffic, in line at the post office, or doing household chores. It will help lower your partner's blood pressure and bind you more tightly together as you take on the drudgery of life.

Finally, your laughter debt will be the most enjoyable and rewarding debt you ever repay. It's a debt that violates the laws of economics: every payment makes you richer rather than poorer.

Keep Things in Perspective

Lighten up! Don't take yourselves too seriously. As a wise person once told us, "You need to keep yourself and what you do and what happens to you in perspective. Don't get caught in the trap of taking yourself too seriously." If one or both of you consistently disregards this piece of wisdom, your relationship can get mired in gloom. Or worse. Consider the experiences of three couples.

Tony and Patti's tenth anniversary was close, and they agreed on a budget to celebrate the event. Patti planned and arranged the celebration. However, she ran slightly over budget. In response, Tony fretted and grumbled incessantly. He kept reminding Patti that they had agreed on the amount to be spent. And she kept telling him that she was doing her best, but that things were more expensive than she had anticipated. Plans for their celebration, as you might expect, soon turned into open warfare.

Tony obviously needed to lighten up and not take his budget so seriously. After all, Patti's overrun was trivial. He would have benefited by following the advice a friend gave us: Never skimp on romance.

Another couple, Leigh and Eric, also struggled from an unhealthy dose of excessive seriousness. Eric, an administrator of a small suburban hospital, went through a dark time when he felt mistreated at work. He complained constantly to Leigh that he wasn't getting the respect he deserved from those he supervised. Leigh tried to bolster his confidence and help him out of his funk, but her attempts were unsuccessful and he continued to feel unappreciated.

It never occurred to Eric that he might be contributing to the problem. He simply blamed his employees for their indifference and disrespect. Eventually, Eric's administrative assistant, who knew of his difficulties, reminded him that respect is something one must earn. Her words unsettled him but caused him to acknowledge that he had made several managerial mistakes. He corrected these and his work situation improved dramatically.

Eric took himself too seriously, thinking that he deserved respect from his workers regardless of how he behaved. As a result, he subjected both Leigh and himself to a long period of emotional distress.

Gail and Luke were plunged into bickering gloom every time they were invited to an event involving his family. The problem had begun during a family dinner at his sister's home. The sister had offered before-dinner drinks to everyone, but somehow overlooked Gail. Despite her sister-in-law's apology, Gail decided she had been intentionally snubbed and decided to avoid further contact with Luke's sister. If she would lighten up and accept her sister-in-law's apology, Gail could shrug off the occurrence and again enjoy family gatherings with her husband.

So lighten up. Don't take yourself so seriously that you get thrown into a black mood by the trivial irritations that are the common lot of us all. The less time you spend in gloom, the more time you are open to laughter.

Create a Laughter-Friendly Environment

Imagine for the moment that laughter is a gift brought to you by an angel. When the angel approaches you, will it encounter a laughter-friendly or a laughter-resistant person? The answer, in large measure, depends on your external and internal environment. For example, we have found that the same movie can be either hilarious or humdrum, depending on whether we are watching it by ourselves or with our sons. They both have a penchant for what we consider "dumb" comedies. For them, the "dumb stuff" is fall-off-the-chair hilarious—and before we know it we get caught up in their fun. Their laughter is contagious. So the first way to create a laughter-friendly environment is to surround yourselves with people who love to laugh.

Second, turn yourselves into laughter-friendly people. Here's a quick test. Which of the following statements is true?

- You smile because you're happy.
- You're happy because you smile.

If you said both are true, you're right. Social psychologists have repeatedly shown that it works both ways: what you do affects how you feel and how you feel affects what you do.[2] If you or your partner is feeling glum, try putting a smile on your face. (However, don't suggest this to someone who is seriously depressed; there are limits to how much you can manipulate your mood.) Smile as you think of the blessings in your life, and work to keep that smile on your face. It will improve your mood. And the more positive your mood, the more receptive you are to laughter.

To some extent, then, if you behave in a way that is consistent with how you want to feel, you can create that feeling. The discovery of this truth was a pleasant surprise to Bart, an electronics engineer. It was Saturday and Bart had accompanied his fiancée, Terry, to an orchid exhibit at a nearby garden. Terry, an avid gardener, was ecstatic. But Bart didn't want to be there. He wanted to get back to work:

"I was behind schedule on a project, and I needed to go to the office even though it was Saturday. The last thing I wanted to do was to traipse around a garden and try to act like I was having fun. I only went because I had promised Terry we'd go, and it was the last day of the exhibit.

"But I was smart enough to know that if I was glum and preoccupied it would be just as bad as if I had cancelled. So I forced myself to smile and look—really look—at the various species of orchids. I had to agree with Terry; they were exotic.

"When we stopped for a picnic lunch, I started to obsess about my project again. But I decided to act like a waiter and serve our lunch with a flourish. Terry started laughing at my antics. Pretty soon, I was laughing, too. The rest of the day, I hardly even thought about work. We both had a great time."

Bart found that by acting in a way he wanted to feel, rather than how he actually felt, his feelings changed. He had, in effect, created a laughter-friendly environment. A potentially bleak experience turned into a memorable event.

Finally, we encourage you to make your physical surroundings as cheerful as possible (we'll talk more about this in Chapter 9). As Viktor Frankl showed, people can still manage to laugh even in the most depressing surroundings. But why put barriers in the way of laughter? If your workplace or home is drab, disorganized, or oppressive, do something to make it more cheerful. Even if you think you are oblivious to such things, spending time in an oppressive atmosphere depresses your mood and makes laughter less likely.

We have found that a well-placed picture or a favorite cartoon can relieve tension and bring a smile to our lips. In our office, we have a wall of self-portraits painted by the special children in our lives. When the work gets tedious or the words fail, these pictures are a perfect antidote. Your surroundings *do* affect your mood.

Raise Your Humor Awareness Level

Yes, the world is filled with struggle and misery and pain. It's also a funny place. So start looking for the humor around you. Remind yourselves to watch for things that bring a smile. You tend to see what you're looking for. In the process, you'll raise your humor awareness level.

As your awareness level goes up, you'll discover the humor in ordinary situations. For example, we stopped in a café for lunch when we were traveling with our daughter in the California wine country. The tables were all taken, so we sat at a lunch counter. Our waitress was not particularly efficient, but she had an infectious laugh and kept making wry comments to us about the food and the customers. We could have focused on the slow service; instead, we relaxed and enjoyed the show. We remember nothing about the food but still treasure the laughter we found in this unexpected place.

You can find humor even in walking your dog. Our friend Bill told us this story:

> "My wife and I had walked longer than we intended and were anxious to get home. As we passed an elderly man and his young grandson, the boy stopped and leaned toward our dog. We have a small terrier who really gets excited around people. I was inclined to pull the leash and hurry on, but I could see that the boy was amused. I decided to stop and let him pet her. She jumped up and down and licked his hand, and he began to cackle. Soon, we were all laughing heartily— the boy at our dog, and the three adults at the boy's infectious laughter."

The incident happened because Bill has a high humor awareness level. Although he wanted to get home, he noted the amused look on the boy's face and responded to it. He and his wife were rewarded with a hearty laugh.

Be a Collector of Humor

As you become more aware of the amusing things around you, remember to share them with each other. Think about it for a moment. Our lives are punctuated with funny words and actions— a joke received over the Internet, the antics of your kids, a clever cartoon in the newspaper, a silly moment at the grocery store, and so on. Yet all too often, they slip from memory before we have a chance to share them. So we urge you to become a collector of humor—to remember and share as many of your laughter experiences as possible with your partner.

You can be a collector of humor in a couple of ways. First, make a mental note of funny incidents and experiences that you can later relate to your partner. The *mental note* is important. How often have you heard someone say, "I just don't remember jokes"? But people can remember anything they choose to remember, and practice makes perfect. The more you are aware that humor can be shared, the more you will remember it. And the more it is shared, the greater the enjoyment. So be on the lookout for jokes and stories you think your partner will like, store them in your memory, and share them when you are together.

Second, you can be a collector in a more literal sense by writing down incidents, clipping cartoons, or keeping a humor folder. If you are an avid collector, you may need more than mental notes. You may want to make notes about the funny things you hear or observe in order to remember them. Include both the things that made you laugh at the time and those that might be something you and your partner can enjoy together. For example, here's a page from one woman's humor notebook:

- Boss sneezed
- Doctor joke
- Worst late-excuse award
- Restaurant clerk
- Vera's boyfriend's zipper
- Radio show

These shorthand notes refer to the following incidents:

- The boss, a very stiff and proper man, sneezed loudly while on the telephone with an important client. Red-faced, he apologized profusely and glanced around the office with clear embarrassment. She didn't laugh at the time, but she and her husband had a hearty laugh about it later.
- A coworker told a doctor joke she thought her husband would like.

- A coworker was late finishing an assignment. He gave what she thought deserved the "worst late-excuse" award, telling his supervisor that he had completely lost track of which day of the week it was because the day indicator on his watch was broken.
- She had lunch with Vera at a fast-food restaurant. The inept cashier botched their order, took it back to correct it, still didn't bring everything they ordered, then glared at them as though they were to blame.
- While at lunch, Vera related a funny story about her boyfriend breaking his zipper so that he couldn't unzip his pants, making restroom visits an acrobatic exercise.
- A radio talk show host made some funny comments on a show she heard on her drive home.

With so many incidents, it would be easy to forget any one of them. If a particular incident is very involved, you may also need to make notes in order to remember the details. It only takes a moment to jot down the notes. The payoff is a healthy round of shared laughter.

Relive Past Times of Laughter

When we hear people discuss what separates humans from other animals, we seldom hear anyone mention an element that we think is crucial—the human capacity for memory. Other animals apparently have some ability to remember; however, only humans seem able to grieve over or laugh about long-past incidents. But notice that you do have the capacity to laugh as well as grieve. You're undoubtedly familiar with the notion of painful memories. What we want you to do is to cultivate and make use of humorous memories.

Laughter from the past can continue to provide enjoyment in the present. For instance, we continue to laugh about the time we'd traveled from the Midwest to research a project at several West Coast libraries. We were staying with friends while we worked on a project at one large California university library. While Jeanette worked at the card catalog, Bob went to the special collections room. There he was told that he would need a pass before he could enter. He went to the counter where passes were issued, but no one was there. After a few more inquiries, someone finally gave him a card to fill out. The card required a local address. Bob knew where our friends lived but couldn't remember the address. He left it blank. The clerk insisted that he provide a number. He pondered the problem. He couldn't look it up in the telephone directory because our friends had an unlisted number. He made up a number and wrote it down. The clerk looked at it and said, "What's the zip code?"

"I don't know," Bob said wearily.

"You have to have a zip code," the clerk persisted. "You can use the zip code directory on the next floor."

Bob trudged up to the area where the directory was located, reached in his pocket for his glasses, and realized that he had left them with Jeanette. He couldn't possibly see the zip code, so he made one up and took the card back.

He watched anxiously as the clerk looked at it, fearful that the young man might find out that the zip code was wrong or even that there was no such address. He breathed a sigh of relief when the clerk issued the pass. Bob found Jeanette, retrieved his glasses, and proceeded to the special collections section. There he pored over a great deal of material, found some old records that were very useful, took them to the lady in charge, and asked where he could copy them. Seemingly amazed at his audacity, she told him in no uncertain terms, "You can't copy those documents."

"Why not? They're so old that there can't be any copyright protection."

She shrugged and pointed to what looked like an ancient stamp on the materials that said they were not to be copied. "What's the use of having them if no one can copy anything from them?" Bob asked.

She just glared at him. "I'm sorry. You can't copy them."

The materials would have been useful for our project. Yet after hours of making up numbers, trying to follow bureaucratic rules, and working through old manuscripts, all we ended up with was a funny memory (though we weren't laughing at the time). It was one of those experiences that are only funny in retrospect. But it *is* funny now, and we continue to enjoy it.

We encourage you to let your humorous memories continue to make you laugh. Keep an active memory bank of funny experiences from your past and relive them together. The experiences will only grow funnier with time.

Be a Producer and Consumer of Humor

When we suggest this, we can count on someone saying, "I can't do that. I'm not a comic. I can collect it, but I can't create it." We disagree. You may not have the potential to be a stand-up comic, but you can be a producer as well as a consumer of humor. As we pointed out in Chapter 2, everyone has creative potential, including the potential to be creative at play. Before you decide against this, read on.

Play Word Games

One way to produce humor is to play word games. The great thing about word games is that they are free, exercise your mind, and can bring laughter to your relationship.

Word games require very little effort. We make a game of observing the literal meaning of people's words. For example, if you eat out you have no doubt heard servers say, "If you need anything, my name is Sarah." We look at each other when Sarah has left and raise the question, "And what do you suppose her name is if we don't need anything?" All you need to do for such a game is listen carefully to what people say and think about a response that would be appropriate to the literal meaning of their words.

Another word game is to make up spoonerisms. Named after an English clergyman who was noted for his verbal slips, a spoonerism involves transposing the initial letters or sounds of two words. Spooner himself is reputed to have looked out at his congregation, lamented the deteriorated state of the pews, and commented: "We must do something about these beery wenches" (a slip for "weary benches"). Thus, we were discussing a story with some friends when the wife grinned and said, "A-ha, the thick plottens."

Still another word game (the possibilities are limitless) is to combine words that would ordinarily not be used together. In lecturing, for instance, we have used such phrases as:

- "He had mastered the art of insensitivity."
- "She was wonderfully oblivious to every negative criticism."
- "He is completely dependable; you can always count on his being late."
- "She suffers from terminal abrasiveness."

Imagine Humorous Possibilities

Look at a situation that is serious or irritating. Then imagine the humorous possibilities and create a funny response. Many situations lend themselves to this exercise. For instance, when a couple cut off by a speeding driver calmed down, the man turned to his wife and said, "I'd love to have a horn that sounds like screeching brakes and another that sounds like a police siren for people like that."

We once worked in a university department where colleagues started giving (privately among ourselves) the "John Doe award" (for obvious reasons, we're not using the person's real name) to the staff person who lasted the longest while doing the least amount of work. "John Doe" had done such a notoriously good job of avoiding anything that resembled a contribution to the goals of the department that his name was a natural for the award.

You can hone your skills at imagining humorous possibilities by taking a situation of your own or by discussing one or more of the following:

- A fitting comeuppance for an in-law whose field of expertise is putting people down
- A career line for a boss whose only concern is to wring every last ounce of productivity from his workers
- The best way to respond to telemarketers who call at dinnertime

Do Takeoffs

This is difficult, but it's a good project for those of you who seriously want to flex your humor muscles. By *takeoffs* we mean to use existing material or ideas and put your own spin on them. For example, you might want to formulate your own takeoff on Murphy's law ("If anything can go wrong, it will"). Yours might read: "Smith's law says that if it's as easy as it looks, you haven't done it right."

Or you might try to make up your own lists of the "ten reasons why . . ." or the "ten best (or worst) . . . " These are not easy, but they are fun to do over dinner. In fact, we've been tempted at times to go over to a restaurant table where a couple looked utterly bored with each other and suggest that they work together on a list of "the ten best moments in our relationship" or "the ten worst things to hear from a waiter."

Choose to See the Humorous Side of Things

Some things are a cinch to make you laugh. Our list includes puns of all kinds, *The New Yorker* cartoons, and the antics of our children and grandchildren. Other things don't carry the same laughter guarantee and can generate a response that ranges anywhere from anger to laughter. Whatever the initial impulse, however, you can choose to see the humorous rather than the dark side of many things. You can laugh rather than get frustrated or angry.

A study at the University of Maryland Medical Center used this idea to examine the deterring effect of laughter on heart attacks.[3] The researchers compared situational responses of 150 people without heart disease to 150 people who had either suffered a heart attack or had bypass surgery. One situation, for example, involved eating in a restaurant with friends. The waiter accidentally spills a drink on you. How would you react? Would you be angry, be amused but not show it, smile, laugh, or laugh heartily?

The researchers found that people with heart disease were less likely to see the humor in such situations or to use humor to relieve the discomfort. They laughed less than those free of heart disease and were more prone to anger and hostility.

We've already made the point that laughter is good for your health. What we want to emphasize here is that you can respond in differing ways to situations. As the participants in the study showed, you can deal with many uncomfortable or distressing situations either by getting angry or by seeing their humorous side.

You and your partner, therefore, need to help each other to see the humorous side of things whenever possible. Obviously, not every situation has a funny side, but many do—including some that make a lot of people very hostile and angry.

Claire tells how her husband, Walt, helped her to laugh rather than cry:

"We had been married only two years, and I was having both our families over for Christmas dinner. Everything seemed to go wrong. First, my oven wouldn't heat. We finally managed to get the turkey over to Walt's brother's house and put it in his oven. Of course, that meant dinner would be late. Then I discovered that Walt had forgotten to buy whipped cream for the pies. The stores were closed, so we'd have to do without. Then the sink stopped up. I'd stuffed too many potato peelings and onion skins down the garbage disposal and it objected. Then my sister, who was supposed to bring the cranberry sauce and a vegetable, called to say they were having car trouble and might not make it.

"At that point, all I wanted to do was to sit down and cry. I was completely frustrated. But Walt knew just what to do. He put his arms around me, smiled, and said: 'You know, in a few days we're going to really find this funny. It'll probably become a family story that we'll laugh about one day with our kids.'

"At first, I just glared at him. I couldn't believe he was taking my crisis so lightly. I wanted to hit him with something. But then I realized that he was trying to console me and help me see that there really was a funny side to my mess. So I shook off my frustrations, and together we did what we could to salvage the dinner. We shared the trials of the day with the family that evening, and everyone had a good laugh as well as a lot of sympathy for me. I guess even a disaster like that can be funny if you keep it in perspective."

Try Going Out of Character

When you go out of character, you depart from your usual, expected behavior. You become, for the moment, a different person. Going out of character to produce a laugh can be something you do alone or together. If you are wondering what exactly it is you do when you go out of character, here are a few examples that people have shared with us:

- "I'm a serious person. My wife is even more serious than I am. So when I think she needs to break out of her seriousness, I first break out of mine. She's always loved the show *Seinfeld* on TV, so I get her to lighten up by whistling the show's theme song and doing a little dance for her. She'll at least crack a smile and usually joins in the dancing."

- "After we've seen a movie, my boyfriend and I like to pretend that we're two of the characters we've just seen on the screen. Then we make up our own story line and change the movie from what it was to something completely dumb."

- "When we were on our honeymoon, my husband would drape a sheet around himself, pretend he was an ancient Roman, and invite me to an orgy. We were like two kids playing together."

- "We like to hide things from each other. One time I did something I wouldn't believe I'd ever do. I hid his wallet in my panties. He looked all over the house before he thought about looking for it on me. When he finally found it . . . well, you can probably guess that it led to more than laughter."

Expect It to Happen

One of the ways to create a good relationship, according to psychotherapist William J. Lederer, is to follow the law of expectations: "When you have *positive* expectations, your behavior assists the event to turn out successfully."[4] Obviously, there are limits to how much your expectations can bring about what you want. However, it's true that if you don't expect much laughter in your relationship you are less likely to have much of it, while if you expect a lot you are more likely to get it.

As Lederer pointed out, your own behavior will help bring about what you desire. This can happen in at least two ways. First, if you expect to laugh with your partner, you will be more alert to funny situations, humorous responses, and opportunities to share humor. Second, your positive attitude will encourage your partner to be more humorous and laugh with you.

So if you are both committed to bringing more laughter into your relationship, don't squelch it with the negative attitude that it probably won't happen:

- "But we're so busy, we don't have time or energy for the task."
- "We'd like it to happen, but we just aren't good at making each other laugh."
- "My partner doesn't have much of a sense of humor."

Such statements reflect the kind of negative expectations that will kill your chances for more laughter.

Follow the ten tips we have discussed. Then expect laughter to happen. And it will.

Play for Keeps

We recently overheard a discussion between a father and his son who were playing doubles in a local tennis tournament. The father was probably in his late fifties and the son in his early twenties. After missing a game-point ball, the son told his father where he should have been in order to make the needed return. The father, somewhat irritated, replied: "I know where I was supposed to be— I just couldn't get there."

We think of this father and his dilemma as a parable for those people who tell us that they know where they ought to be in terms of laughter in their relationship, but they just can't get there. Our hope is that the ten tips we offered in this chapter will provide some useful suggestions for you.

If you think you're too busy or too serious or too inept or too whatever else to bring more laughter into your relationship, we recommend that you start with something simple. For example, how about working together for the next week to enhance your humor awareness? As you each go about your daily activities, watch for funny happenings. Listen to the words people use, watch their expressions, be alert to their antics. Also be aware of the things you say and do; you may be a lot funnier than you think. Then share the humor you have discovered with your partner. We've found that dinner is a good time to do this. It's a great way to reconnect at the end of the day. Plus, it'll work wonders for your digestion.

If you think that your humor awareness is already well developed, you might prefer to work on one of the other ways discussed in this chapter. In any case, do *something*. Make a start at paying off your lifelong laughter debt.

6

Spur-of-the-Moment
Play

We were on a research trip, investigating sexual and family practices in American utopian communities. We had allotted a couple of months to complete the study, and time was growing short. The last leg of our journey was in New York, where we had a tight schedule of places to visit. Driving north toward Chatham, we noticed a sign indicating an approaching turnoff to Hyde Park, the site of Franklin D. Roosevelt's home. We both love history and have visited most of the presidential sites in the nation, but we had never been to Hyde Park.

There we were, torn between our schedule and our desire to visit Hyde Park, with little time to evaluate our options. On the spur of the moment, we opted for Hyde Park, a decision that put us two days behind schedule. At the time, we had no regrets. Today, we still have no regrets—unless it's the regret of not having gone with our whims more often. The experience taught us the value of spur-of-the-moment play, the spontaneous fun that can occur at any time, including times when other things are already scheduled.

The point is, don't think of spur-of-the-moment play as something you do only when nothing else is scheduled. Spur-of-the-moment play occurs any time you engage in fun that you hadn't planned. It can occur on a vacation when you make a spontaneous change in your plans, or it can occur in the midst of a tight schedule when you spontaneously take a break.

Spur-of-the-moment play is easier for some people than for others. Those who go with the flow, who enjoy the process more than reaching the goal, revel in spur-of-the-moment play more so than those who are goal oriented and need closure on their activities.[1] Unfortunately, more Americans (including us) fall into the latter than the former category. For most of us, spur-of-the-moment play is more likely resisted than embraced. We'd like to persuade you, nevertheless, to become an "embracer."

Are You Spontaneous?

Children provide the best examples of being spontaneous in play. Most children easily engage in spur-of-the-moment play, as anyone knows who has tried to pass a playground without letting a child in hand stop to play. In fact, the *lack* of spontaneous play is one sign of a troubled child. More often, if you're an adult, it's a sign that you've succumbed to the compelling reasons for *not* engaging in spur-of-the-moment play. And there is, as it happens, no shortage of convincing reasons.

Why Not?

Even if you admire the ability of children to be spontaneous in play, you can always muster up a list of reasons why you shouldn't opt for spur-of-the-moment play at a given time. As we write this, for example, we can come up with our own list:

- The deadline for the completion of this book is close at hand.

- The chapter we are currently working on is moving along well, so we shouldn't interrupt our progress.
- To continue working is the responsible, adult course of action.
- We both have a strong need for getting a job done promptly; to take a break now would go against that need.
- It may be true that all work and no play makes Jack a dull boy, but all play and no work makes Bob and Jeanette a financially strapped and professionally impoverished couple.

Need we add more? You could draw up a similar list for yourself whenever you have an itch to play instead of work. We know the power of those reasons. We acknowledge that more often than not, we have resisted the temptation to just take off and do something fun because we had responsibilities that took priority over our impulses.

We are not advocating that you always follow your whims. We don't encourage you to strive to become more irresponsible adults. But it's probable that in the matter of spur-of-the-moment play you err on the side of caution rather than the side of abandon. Most couples we know practice the "work before play" adage with a vengeance.

A Spontaneity Quiz

How open are you to spur-of-the-moment play? How spontaneous are you as a couple? Take the following test to find out. In the situations that follow, assuming that in each case the spur-of-the-moment option appeals to you both, how likely is it that you would go for it?

- Saturday morning is the time you regularly do chores around the house. It's a beautiful spring day. You look at each other and agree it would be great to take the morning off and do something fun. What do you do?

- It's late. You both feel sexually aroused. But you both also have important meetings tomorrow and need a good night's sleep. What do you do?
- You are on a tight budget. You notice that a favorite group is giving a concert in your city next month. You would love to attend, but the ticket prices are beyond your recreational budget. You have only a short time to decide, because the concert will be sold out quickly. What do you do?
- You are eating in a restaurant that features live music. You realize that the combo is playing "your" song—the one you danced to at your wedding. There is a small space where people can dance, though there's no one dancing at the time. It could be a magical moment for you, but you're not sure if the restaurant really encourages dancing. What do you do?

If these are not the kinds of situations you might find yourself in, make up some of your own. Test yourself. Be as honest as you can about how much spontaneity there is in your couple play. We suspect that you'll want to increase the amount.

Spontaneity Adds a Special Sizzle

There's a good reason for indulging spur-of-the-moment impulses and engaging in spontaneous play: it adds a special sizzle to your relationship. In spontaneous play you not only gain the benefits of regular play, but you add a sense of daring and anticipation. Consider the following two accounts. The first is from a woman married ten years:

"There are a lot of things I admire and love about Martin. But if I were going to change one thing, I would like to make him less predictable. Not unpredictable, of course. Just *less* predictable. I'd just like to see him do something a little screwy, a little off-the-wall, once in a while."

The second is from Alex, whose marriage to Kay has been a "seven-year adventure":

"Kay is quirky. She's never been afraid to be unconventional. We were watching children splash in a fountain once and she took off her shoes and jumped in with them. The children loved it. So did she. And so did I. I didn't go in, but I still found it great fun.

"From time to time, Kay will suggest we do something that really tests my flexibility. Like the time she dared me to pack our suitcases and just take off for a few days. 'Where will we go?' I asked her. 'Let's just drive north and see what appeals,' she said. 'But we're supposed to meet your parents for dinner tomorrow night,' I reminded her. She said she'd call them and reschedule. So we did it! We felt like a couple of naughty kids, but we had a blast."

As Alex's account illustrates, spur-of-the-moment play adds a special sizzle to your relationship. Each new day promises the potential of adventure and surprise. It may be a trip, like Alex and Kay took, or just a few moments when you engage in playful behavior with each other. In either case, you are on a joyride together.

Give Yourselves Permission

As we noted earlier, there are always convincing reasons for *not* engaging in spur-of-the-moment play. Unfortunately, most people are convinced too much of the time. It seems like they almost instinctively suppress or say no to the impulse to play. If you're one of these people, what can you do to bring more fun into your life?

You begin by giving yourselves permission. First, remind yourselves of the value of spur-of-the-moment play. Second, agree with each other that you will let it happen. And, third, avoid knee-jerk decisions.

Remind Yourselves of the Value of
Spur-of-the-Moment Play

We've already noted two reasons that spur-of-the-moment play is valuable:

- It yields the same benefits as other kinds of play.
- It has the additional benefit of adding an element of daring and anticipation to your relationship.

In addition, spur-of-the-moment play helps you live in the present. Living in the present moment means to be absorbed in where you are and what you're doing. Such absorption is key to reaping the full benefits of any activity. Psychiatrist Harold Bloomfield insisted that you can find ecstasy even in something like doing the dishes because:

> The key to ecstasy in whatever you are doing is to allow yourself to be fully engaged in doing it. That means: *not complaining* to yourself about it, *not worrying* about how long it'll take, *not planning* what you'll do when it is over, *not watching* yourself to see how well you're doing . . . letting your feelings, thoughts, and movements blend in one graceful flow of activity.[2]

How often are you absorbed like this? You may be working, for example, but thinking about what you will do when you get home. You may be reading to your child but thinking about work. You may even be playing but thinking about something else. More than once, we've been at a movie or play that wasn't engaging and found ourselves thinking about what we would have for dinner afterward. But when you are engaged in true play, you are living in the present moment—fully engaged with and absorbed by the activity. Alex describes it well:

> "You remember that saying about taking time to smell the roses? It's right on. It really hit me one day how many times—metaphorically

speaking—I've passed roses in my life without smelling them. That's one of the things I love about Kay. She'll always stop. And that causes me to stop. And every time I do, I think: 'This is what life is about. This is really living.'"

Agree to Let It Happen

This means that you agree not to automatically say no to an impulse to engage in spur-of-the-moment play because it appears foolish or irresponsible, or for any other of the "good reasons" you might come up with. Agree that at times you will let it happen, even if the good reasons are compelling.

For example, there are times when spur-of-the-moment play involves something that an outsider might see as foolish. When Kay jumped into the fountain and joined the children as they cavorted in the water, some passersby shot her disapproving looks. To them, she looked ridiculous—she wasn't "acting her age." Fortunately, Alex saw the event for what it was—a spontaneous, joyous response to a group of playing children.

There may be times when spur-of-the-moment play appears irresponsible. A few years ago we were vacationing in Canada and purchased nonrefundable tickets for a play. As the time for the play approached, we found something else we wanted to do. As usual, there were a number of good reasons for going to the play rather than the spur-of-the-moment alternative:

- We wouldn't be able to get our money back.
- We don't like to think of ourselves as people who can't make up their minds and are tossed about by every whim.
- The play might turn out to be better than the alternative in the long run.

But we went with our impulse and skipped the play. And the outcome? We made the right decision!

Avoid Knee-Jerk Decisions

Clearly, we gave the matter some thought before opting out of the play. Spontaneous doesn't mean mindless or instantaneous. Kay's decision to frolic in the water was close to being instantaneous. ("I did hesitate a moment," she admitted, "but decided to throw caution to the wind and join the kids.")

Knee-jerk means you give no thought at all to a decision. When the whim comes, you automatically reject or accept it. This is not a healthy reaction. Even if you have agreed to let spur-of-the-moment play happen, this doesn't mean you must go with every impulse. There are times when you *should* say no.

For instance, when Alex and Kay were walking the beach on a Caribbean vacation, they passed a booth that rented snorkeling equipment. "Wow," Kay exclaimed, "wouldn't that be fun? Let's do it." She knew that Alex didn't swim well and that he feared having his head under water because of a traumatic childhood incident. But she kept cajoling him until he reluctantly gave in. He didn't want to pass up an opportunity to smell the roses because of his fears.

Although Kay was initially exuberant, she soon wished she hadn't been so insistent:

> "Well, that's one battle that I thought I'd won but really lost. I kept telling Alex not to be so nervous, that once he got in the water he would love it and want to do it again. But he didn't love it and we've not done it again. He panicked when a wave swept over us and carried him along. He swallowed a mouthful of water, choked, and headed quickly for shore. It was a disaster. Alex was mortified by his reaction, and I felt guilty that I had insisted that he do it."

Kay made the mistake of a knee-jerk reaction. She never considered the possibility that it might be better to say no to the activity. She couldn't imagine that something that appealed so much to her might be no fun at all for him.

The same rule applies to spur-of-the-moment play as to all other play: it's not really play unless you're both enjoying it. This means that you don't coerce your partner into doing something on the grounds that you *know* he or she will enjoy it. Granted, you might be right. But more often than not, you'll be wrong. And the experience will be one you'll put in the loss column of your relationship.

So with this caveat in mind, we encourage you to take the first step in adding more spur-of-the-moment play to your relationship—give yourselves permission. The second step involves what we call *getting in touch with your inner clown.*

Get in Touch with Your Inner Clown

We watched as a distinguished-looking man and a small boy—we decided they were grandfather and grandson—came into a fast-food restaurant for lunch. They took their food to a table next to ours and began to eat. We couldn't help but notice (nosy observers of the human species that we are) that the grandfather was relating a tall tale, using different voices and making funny faces for the characters in the story. The little boy roared. It was obvious that he was delighted with his grandfather's performance. When the tale ended, we heard him beg his grandfather for "just one more story."

What this grandfather did for his grandson, you can do for each other. That is, you can get in touch with your inner clown and be silly for each other. Silliness is one of the more common forms of spur-of-the-moment play. We have yet to meet a child who didn't have the capacity to be silly. And as the grandfather illustrated, that capacity remains with people throughout their lives. It can be suppressed, but never killed.

Indeed, we would take it a step farther. We believe that adults *need* to be silly on occasion. A little silliness keeps you from taking yourselves too seriously, allows you to express the fun-loving child that is still within you, and adds glue to your relationship. As two counselors described it in terms of their own marriage,

> "The capacity to be silly with each other is an index of the level of trust in our marriage. We are not likely to play in an atmosphere that isn't safe. We have to feel at home to let our child out and act the part of the fool."[3]

Silliness Is . . .

Just what does it mean to be silly? It means many different things. Here are a few examples:

- "Ken and I were eating dinner with a number of other couples. It was a pretty stuffy affair. I was sitting across the table from Ken. I glanced over at him and he crossed his eyes at me. He then looked away and kept eating without missing a beat. I soon caught his attention and crossed my eyes back at him. We kept it up through most of the dinner—being careful, of course, that no one was watching. But we both almost lost it at times. And afterward, when we were alone, we laughed until our sides hurt."
- "Jan and I were walking along on a sidewalk when I remembered how my father had played this game with me when I was young. I impulsively said to Jan, 'I bet I can make you step on a line.' She looked puzzled. I pointed to the lines in the sidewalk and repeated my challenge. 'I'll bet you can't,' she said. So we went to the end of the block with me pulling her, stopping, then pushing and pulling some more to make her step on a line. She was better at it than I had been with my father. She kept giving me the V-sign and her victory grin the rest of the day."
- "I don't remember how it got started, but every so often when one of us wants to do something and the other

doesn't, the one who wants to do it will go into a child's snit. And the other one will take the part of a determined parent. Sometimes we wind up doing the thing and sometimes we don't, but we always have fun working it out by being silly."

- "When Hope and I were first married, we saw a movie where this pouting actress lay on a couch and complained about her life. One night when we were sitting at home in our living room and feeling a bit bored, Hope said, 'Remember this?' Then she draped herself on the couch and went through that routine. I laughed and laughed at her. It turned a dull evening into one I'll always remember."

There are many other ways couples act silly together. What works for other couples may not work for you. To find out what *does* work for you, you need to discover what kind of clown you each have within you.

Find Out What Kind of Clown You Are

Some people are, by temperament, more outgoing than others. Some are more introverted. Some are bolder, others more reserved. We are not suggesting that, regardless of your personality, you turn into a stand-up comic. At the same time, whether your natural tendency is to be outgoing or shy, lighthearted or serious, there is some kind of clown within you. You *do* have the capacity to be silly with your partner. The challenge is to find out what kind of clown you are and to set your clown free.

How do you get in touch with your inner clown? Begin by talking with your partner about past "performances." How many times do you recall being silly together? What did each of you do? Perhaps one of you was the clown and the other was the audience, as with Hope and her husband. Or perhaps you engaged in joint silliness, like the couple who crossed their eyes at each other during the formal dinner.

As you do this, you'll gain some insight into the kinds of silliness that come to you naturally and that you each find pleasing. Follow your discussion with a laugh contest. The idea is for one of you to do or say something that will make the other laugh. When you succeed, change roles. If you want to make it a true contest, time each other to see who takes the longest to make the other laugh.

The purpose of this exercise, of course, is to free your inner clowns. Hopefully, engaging in this bit of silliness will free you for more in the future. But remember that there are many forces that can suppress inner clowns. So repeat the exercise whenever you hit a dry spell of seriousness.

Think Small

A third step in adding more spur-of-the-moment play to your relationship is to think small. Recognize that spur-of-the-moment play is much more likely to happen if you think of it as something that is readily accessible rather than as something dramatic. Chad put it this way:

"I used to think of being spontaneous in terms of something spectacular. Like the guy I read about who 'kidnapped' his wife and took her away for a romantic weekend. I thought this was really daring. I imagined how much fun it would be to surprise Zoe by spiriting her off to Paris for dinner and dancing—you know, like rich people do in the movies.

"But one day we were working in our garden when Zoe accidentally sprayed me with the hose. When I yelled, she giggled and sprayed me some more. I ran into the house to prevent a full-scale water war. She stood outside and laughed. And it hit me. That's being spontaneous! You can do it anywhere! Any time! It doesn't have to be something spectacular or expensive to be a lot of fun!"

Chad realized after this incident that spur-of-the-moment play can take place in the ordinary and the routine. We'll explore this idea in greater detail in Chapter 9.

Think Surprise

A final step you can take to increase your spur-of-the-moment play is to think surprise. That is, plan ways to surprise your partner. "Wait a minute," you say, "Isn't 'planned spontaneity' a contradiction in terms?" Yes and no. If you plan together, it's clearly not spur-of-the-moment play. But if one of you plans a surprise, it has the effect of being spontaneous for your partner.

How Do You Surprise?

You surprise your partner any time you play in an unexpected way. As the following examples show, surprises range from the simple to the elaborate:

- "When a friend first introduced Molly to me, I didn't catch her name. 'Mopsy?' I asked her. Everyone laughed. I knew right away that I was remembering a rabbit's name from a children's story. But Molly really liked it. It became my private nickname for her even before we were married. One day I opened my underwear drawer and was startled to see a pair of pink panties appliquéd with the name 'Mopsy' and several little bunnies. I've left them there. Every time I open the drawer, it reminds me of what a special wife I have."
- "On a scale that runs from least likely to most likely to surprise you, Trevor is closer to the 'least likely' end. But he *does* surprise me at times. Like once I came home to a dozen red roses with a note that said, 'Just because I love you.' I

was flabbergasted. He never brings me flowers. My first reaction was to ask him what he was apologizing for. But it turned out to be just a surprise gift he'd gotten on impulse. I love it when he does things like that."

- "For our tenth anniversary, I thought we should do something special. Beth told me that she wanted to plan the whole thing and wanted it to be a surprise. The only thing she told me was to dress for dinner. So I figured that we were going to a really fancy restaurant. But it turned out to be one surprise after another. First, a limo picked us up at our front door. I'd never been in one before. We were driven to the bay, where a gondola was waiting for us. That was the second surprise. The third was drinking champagne in the gondola while the gondolier sang Italian love songs. After that we were taken to dinner, and finally the limo drove us back home. It was the most fantastic evening ever."

- "I took off work early and prepared a candlelight dinner for the two of us."

- I had to take an early flight so I wrote 'I love you' on the bathroom mirror with toothpaste. I wanted it to be the first thing she saw when she got up in the morning."

Surprise Is Sharp-Edged Fun

Whether simple and easy or dramatic and complicated, surprises are what we call *sharp-edged* fun. When couple play includes the unexpected, intensity is added to the experience. Surprises create a surge of emotion, a rush of feeling that lingers on through the whole play experience and often for a long time afterward.

We learned this on a memorable day in New Hampshire. We were in Concord, the capital, for a few days. As we left our motel one morning to drive to the Franklin Pierce home (as we noted earlier, we love history), we noticed a brochure about a nearby winery. It claimed to be the northernmost grape winery in New England. This was an unexpected find (we also love to visit small wineries), and putting a visit to the winery on the day's agenda added a measure of delightful anticipation.

When we arrived at the Franklin Pierce home, we were disappointed to find it closed for the day. "Well," said Bob, "we're at least going to get a picture." Jeanette stood on the steps of the home while Bob took her picture. As we were leaving, an elderly man opened the door and called out to us. He was the docent (museum guide). He explained that the home was closed because the local historical society was meeting there that day. "Would you like to see the house?" he asked. "The meeting won't start for a little while."

We had a delightful personal tour by a man who clearly loved the home and loved showing it. At the end of our visit, he urged us to go to the workshop of a pewter artisan. "It's on your way," he said. "I know you'll enjoy it."

As we drove away, we debated whether to take the time to stop at the artisan's shop. We decided to go for it and, as a result, spent nearly an hour with an enchanting man. He was a retired minister who had fallen in love with handcrafted pewter art and trained to become a master artisan. An exhibit of his art at the Boston Museum of Fine Art testified to the success of his venture.

Our final stop was the winery, where the owner invited us to tour his facility. He spoke with pride and enthusiasm as he showed us his equipment, described the wine-making and bottling process, and let us sample his product.

We have been on many house tours and have visited numerous wineries. We have chatted with many artists. But that day in New Hampshire is high on our list of the best of times. Again and again, we came face to face with the unexpected. What began as a visit to a historic home turned into three adventures. We met three men thoroughly in love with what they were doing. At each place, we were treated as honored guests. And at each place the unexpected passion of the men for their work intensified both our interest in and our enjoyment of what they were doing. The sharp-edged pleasure of the day remains with us years afterward.

In this case, the surprises came from others. What these men did for us, you can do for each other. And each time you do, you'll give your partner a measure of sharp-edged fun.

Surprise Is a Message of Love

In addition to being sharp-edged fun, a surprise is a message of love. Whether your surprise is simple or elaborate, it sends your partner an important message—or, more accurately, a set of messages:

- I think about you.
- I want to please you.
- I have given thought and time to an act that will bring you pleasure.
- And all of this is because I love you and cherish our relationship.

Bobbi is a college administrator who deals with many stressful situations. Her message of love came after she felt emotionally drained by an incident involving the sexual harassment of a student by a professor:

"Joe knew I needed a break from it all. The prof was a friend of mine, which made it doubly painful. I came home one Friday evening, while the investigation was still going on, feeling physically, mentally, and emotionally low. On the kitchen counter I found three envelopes. 'Open this first' was written on the top one. I opened it and found a brief note of support and love from Joe. In the second, I read that I was to take a long bath and that dinner would arrive by delivery service later when he got home from the office. And the third one informed me that I had an appointment for an hourlong massage the next morning.

"The bath and dinner and massage were wonderful. But the most wonderful thing of all was realizing how much Joe loves me for him to go to so much trouble."

Think surprise. Do the unexpected for your partner. It will not only be sharp-edged fun, but it will send a message of love.

Play for Keeps

In order for you to develop the spontaneous side of your nature, we recommend that you declare a *PS (planned spontaneity) month*. Select a month or a four-week period in the near future that will be your PS month. During the month, plan a surprise for your partner every week and be alert for opportunities to engage in spur-of-the-moment play.

The point of designating a PS month is to make spur-of-the-moment play salient in your mind and to ensure that you will experience a surprise as one form of such play. We believe that the greatest hindrance to spur-of-the-moment play—next to the sound, practical reasons that always come to mind—is the tendency to be absorbed in serious thoughts. If you keep in mind that it's PS month, you will be alert for opportunities for spur-of-the-moment play. And having practiced it for a month, you are likely to have more of it in the future.

Don't make the surprise so elaborate that it becomes impractical. We don't discourage you from a dramatic surprise if you have the resources, but keep in mind that surprises can be simple. Here are some examples:

- Write and mail your partner a letter telling why you value your relationship.
- At an unexpected time, give your partner a hug and kiss and say, "I love you."
- Call your partner at work and give him or her a love message.
- Buy a small gift (for example, a book, a CD, or candy) and present it with a love note.
- Write your partner a poem.
- Plan a date where you go somewhere or do something that has special romantic meaning for the two of you.
- Prepare breakfast in bed for your partner.
- Give your partner a gift certificate for his or her favorite store.

If none of these suggestions grabs you, come up with something else to surprise your partner. The possibilities are endless.

Love Play

Woody Allen once observed that the only bad sex is no sex. Actually, as any marriage counselor or therapist knows, there is a great deal of bad sex. Any kind of sexual behavior that is a disruptive rather than a bonding force in a relationship is bad sex. For it to be good, sex needs to be an integral part of your love play. As psychiatrist R. William Betcher pointed out, the association of playfulness with sexual love goes back at least as far as the ancient Greeks.[1] The god Eros, whose arrows of love could turn even Stoic philosophers into lusting men, went about his work in a playful, capricious way.

Love play includes those behaviors that express affection and passion. These range from sexual innuendoes to flirtatious looks, from stolen moments together to elaborate romantic dates, from tender touches to sexual intercourse. The effectiveness of such love play depends on certain other behaviors, like handling conflict satisfactorily, maintaining personal hygiene, and ongoing individual growth. For this reason, you need to *enlarge your notion of foreplay.*

Enlarge Your Notion of Foreplay

We believe that everything in your life together as a couple is foreplay. The way you treat each other, the things you say to each other, the nonverbal signals you send each other—these all stimulate or dull your appetite for love play. In our work with couples, we have identified three aspects of an intimate relationship that are particularly important as a foundation for love play: the way you handle disagreements, the extent to which you court each other, and the number of loving connections you make with each other.

Handle Disagreements Lovingly

Every couple experiences conflict. In a successful relationship, conflict tends to diminish over time, but it doesn't totally disappear. A study of lasting marriages reported that 12 percent of husbands and wives recalled *major* conflicts early in their marriages, compared to 29 percent during the child-rearing years, and 7 percent during the empty-nest phase.[2] Minor conflicts occurred more often. Whether they're about money, sex, children, your partner's annoying habits, attitudes toward in-laws, or a multitude of other possible issues, you *will* have disagreements that result in major or minor conflicts.

As marital experts point out, when you do have an argument, the method you use to handle it is crucial to the quality of your relationship.[3] The way you deal with each other in resolving an issue will make you feel more or less playful toward your partner and will either cool or intensify your passion for one another. Here are two examples that show contrasting methods and outcomes:

- "Whenever we argue, Kirk puts me down. He belittles what I think and say. And he usually winds up having the last word because I finally give in. Then he wants to kiss and make up. I can tell you that the last thing I want to do is to kiss him after I've been humiliated by his cutting remarks. I just can't do it."
- "Both Robin and I hate conflict. But when we do argue, we try to be considerate of each other's opinion, to really listen

to what the other is saying. So even though it's painful for both of us, we're able to work through a disagreement and actually feel better about our marriage. Sometimes it even acts as an aphrodisiac and we make really sweet love."

These two couples handle arguments in differing ways and experience very different outcomes. The second couple has a solid marriage. The last we heard from the first couple, they were living in a cold war—sleeping in separate bedrooms and spending little time together.

The first couple uses what we call an *attack/defend method* to deal with their disagreements: they each attack the other's position and defend their own until one gives up (usually, as Kirk's wife pointed out, she's the one who surrenders). The second couple uses a loving method, striving to understand and care about each other's position, discussing and negotiating until they are both satisfied with the resolution.

There is no *one* right way for all couples to resolve their differences. It is crucial, however, that you and your partner are both satisfied with the method you use as well as with its outcomes. Otherwise, as with the first couple, your disagreements will be the death of intimacy and love play between you.

Continue to Court One Another

Although it sounds old-fashioned and is seldom used anymore, you know what the word *courting* means. More important, you've experienced it—like those times when your partner tries to please you, to impress you, and to make clear the depth of his or her feelings for you. Unfortunately, if you're married or living together, you have probably also experienced what tends to happen during the first year of sharing the same home—namely, a decline in the frequency with which your partner:

- Compliments you
- Does or says something that makes you laugh
- Says "I love you"
- Takes the initiative in having sex with you
- Does something nice for you
- Is physically affectionate
- Discusses how he or she feels about various matters, and talks about the day's experiences with you[4]

Each of these is a feature of courting behavior. Each is the kind of thing people do when they want to score points with someone and build a lasting, intimate relationship. And each tends to occur less frequently (although not disappear altogether) during the first year of living together. This isn't good foreplay.

Of course, you can't continue to put the same time and energy into courting behavior that you did when you set out to win your partner. A young husband put it this way:

> "When I knew that I wanted to marry Julie, I got a little crazy. I'd leave the office early and even occasionally take off in the afternoon so that I could spend more time with her. I wrote her love letters on office time. I spent so much money on gifts and dates that I'd be bankrupt today if I'd kept it up. And that's the point. You can't keep doing those things."

Yes and no. You can't keep doing them at the same pace, but you *can* and *must* continue doing them. If you're not convinced, try courting each other again for the next three days and see what happens. Commit yourselves to do four or five things each day that you know will please your partner.

What to do? Start with those things we just listed that decline in the first year. Or reprise some of the things you did early in your relationship. When you talk together, hang on your partner's words—

listen and respond. Attend to your partner, extend common courtesies, find ways to please him or her—just the kinds of things that you did when you were wooing him or her. If you both commit to three days of courting, your relationship will be recharged. It never fails.

Make Frequent Loving Connections

Over and again, we hear this complaint from women: "I can't turn on sexually the way my husband can. After we've gone our separate ways all day, I can't turn into an instantaneous sex bomb. I need to reconnect with him first."

And this from the other half of the relationship: "There are times when our schedules are so hectic that we just aren't able to connect the way she wants. Anyway, I don't know of a better way to connect than to have sex. It always makes me feel closer to her."

Here's the dilemma: men need sex to feel connected and women need to be connected to feel sexy. But there is a way out of the quandary. You can stay connected even when you're apart. Some of the things that couples do to stay connected include:

- Leaving brief love messages on their partner's office voice mail
- Putting love notes somewhere their partner will find them—in the refrigerator, a pocket, a briefcase, or purse
- Agreeing to think loving thoughts of each other at a particular time each day
- Faxing or E-mailing love notes

Love notes, incidentally, can be anything from a straightforward "I love you" to various kinds of affirmations: "You're the greatest," "You make me feel good about myself," "I love the way you smile at me," and so forth.

Face-to-face connections are also needed, of course. Liz and Parker have found a way to do this even though they have two school-age children:

> "We take a half-hour after dinner each evening to drink coffee and talk. It's our special time together. When we started doing this a couple of years ago, the kids would interrupt and demand our attention. But we've taught them to respect this time and to leave us alone unless it's an emergency.
>
> "We talk about what's happened during the day, how things are going in our lives, how to deal with various demands and problems we face, and whatever else we want to share with each other. It's a time for us to catch up with each other and really connect at the end of a busy day. These thirty minutes keep us close and remind us that we are a couple."

Such loving connections, combined with courting behavior and a satisfying way of handling differences, provide fertile ground in which love play flourishes.

Give Each Other Love Surprises

Recall that surprises add a sharp edge to your fun together. Love surprises, therefore, are one of the more enjoyable forms of love play. They include surprises of both affection and sex.

Give Affection Surprises

We've already mentioned some affection surprises, such as the unexpected love note in the briefcase or pocket. Here are a few more examples:

- "We were sitting across from each other at dinner at a friend's house. Suddenly I felt her foot rubbing up and down my calf. I looked at her and she smiled with that 'I love you' smile of hers. It was a magical moment!"

- "I just love it when he sneaks up behind me and kisses me on the back of my neck. It always surprises me. And always thrills me."

- "It was our twenty-fifth anniversary, and do you know what he did? He got down on his knees and asked me if I would marry him for another twenty-five years. When I said yes, he pulled out a diamond ring to go with my wedding band. I can't remember a happier moment in my life."

As these illustrate, giving affection surprises is like purchasing a rapidly growing stock: your investment of time and energy yields rich dividends for your relationship. And please note that we have made a distinction between affection surprises and sex surprises. It is particularly important that affection surprises not be limited to those times when one of you desires sex. Paula and Hank's marriage is the second for each of them. Paula loves having sex with Hank, even though her first marriage brought her little sexual satisfaction:

"We do a lot of touching—hugging, holding hands, kissing. And not just when we have sex. My ex, on the other hand, was only affectionate when he wanted sex. It made me resent sex as well as my ex."

In contrast to her first husband, Hank gives Paula many affection surprises "just to let me know how much he loves me. Is it any wonder I can't get enough of that man?"

Give Sex Surprises

A sex surprise is some kind of sexual treat you offer your partner. It may involve an invitation to sex, a special sexual experience, or something unexpected during sex. Here are some of the creative ways people give sex surprises to their partners.

- "We were watching a romantic movie on TV one night. At the end, Taylor said, 'I'm going to take a bath.' 'OK,' I said. 'Why don't you join me?' she asked. She didn't have to repeat the request."
- "It happened at a time when I thought our sex life was getting a little routine. We were on a vacation trip, and I was feeling the need for sex. But I wanted it to be something different. Would you believe it? One evening he tells me he had bought a copy of the *Kama Sutra,* that sex book from India. He asked me if I'd like for him to show me something he had learned from reading it. That was the beginning of a whole new phase in our sex life."
- "Maggie hardly ever takes the initiative in sex. So she really bowled me over one evening when I came home from work. I noticed she had her housecoat on. I thought it was strange but didn't say anything. We talked a little bit, then I asked her what we were going to do for dinner. 'Well,' she said, 'I thought we'd go out. But I thought you might like to have appetizers first.' And with that she opened her housecoat. She didn't have a stitch of clothing on under it."

Obviously, you can't pull off such a surprise every time or even most of the time you have sex. But think about the difference between one of these scenarios and one where the partner simply says to the other, "Wanna have sex tonight?" As with all play, the element of surprise adds an intensity to your pleasure.

One other kind of surprise is to suggest sex at a time when neither of you would ordinarily consider it. Often, that means a "quickie." Hank and Paula had a quickie when they were getting ready to go out with some friends:

"Hank had just gotten out of the shower, and I was shaving my legs. On an impulse, I reached over and gave his butt a love bite. He stopped dead in his tracks. Then he did the same to me. We looked at each other for a moment, grinned, then hopped into bed for a hurry-up sexual encounter before getting dressed and going out with our friends."

We don't recommend quickies as standard fare. True, they satisfy your physical urges, but sex is more than physical. As two experts put it: "When two bodies belonging to two intertwined lives join in an act of sex, much more than physical sensations gets expressed."[5] In addition to the physical aspect, sex, the researchers point out, is also an act in which you disclose something about yourself, engage in intimacy, affirm affection and love, declare your interdependence, and maintain your relationship. Some of these elements get short-changed in a quickie.

Nevertheless, an occasional quickie, in which one partner surprises the other by suggesting sex at an unusual time or place, is one more pleasurable item in your treasure chest of shared bonding experiences.

Plan Love Feasts

A quickie can be good, but it isn't likely to be memorable. If you want to have a memorable experience of love play, plan a love feast. What exactly is a love feast? It's whatever you want it to be. Here are some items on the menu of a love feast from which you can choose (you can add whatever you want to the menu).

Appetizers

- Laughter (go to or rent a funny movie, go to a comedy show, read a book of cartoons together, or find other ways to laugh together)
- Indulgence (pamper yourselves with a long slow bath or shower together)

- Palate pleasure (have a leisurely meal that features your favorite foods)

Main Course

- Sensual stimulation (light candles; spray your favorite scent; turn on some romantic music; give each other a massage; engage in a lot of touching; spend more time than usual in various kinds of foreplay)
- Sexual adventure (try a new position or a new way to stimulate or please each other; if you need help or ideas, a bookstore will provide ample resources)

Dessert

- Pillow talk (whisper sweet nothings; talk about your love feast and how it makes you feel about each other)
- Caressing (*afterplay* is as important as foreplay: caress, embrace, and kiss as a way to affirm that your affection is more than preparation for sex; if you're ready for a second helping of the main course, go for it)

Clearly, the point of a love feast is to immerse yourselves in each other for a period of time. To make it truly a feast, you must not allow yourselves to be distracted by other concerns, whether work, children, in-laws, the budget, or anything else that is bothersome to you. Give yourselves wholly to each other and to shared pleasure. In short, relax and have fun as though you were on your honeymoon.

Planning Your Love Feast

Clearly, to do it right, a love feast requires a block of time. If possible, we recommend that you send the kids to Grandma's for the night or that you plan a weekend away. Psychiatrist William Betcher tells of a couple married twenty-one years who regularly take a week's vacation without their children.[6] The wife told him that the week is "always magical and always involves a lot of play, especially sexually." They choose a place where they can relax rather than sightsee. They frequently pretend they're a newly married couple or a man and a woman having an illicit affair. They do everything at a slow pace and resist any attempts by other people to get involved with them. They focus totally on each other for the entire week.

When you plan your love feast, therefore, do it in a way that allows you to give yourselves wholly to each other. This means:

- Take as much time as you can, but not so much that you feel you are neglecting other matters.
- Go away from home, where it's easier to avoid distractions and responsibilities. But if you can't afford to go away, plan a love feast at home; to paraphrase the poet, it's better to have a love feast at home than never to have a love feast at all.
- Remember, *carefree* is the watchword for your love feast. So if you go away, don't choose a hard-to-get-to place that will take too much travel time, or a too-expensive place where you will be concerned about the cost.
- Plan in advance to make your love feast a carefree time. Your planning may include arranging for child care, finding the right place to stay, or buying erotic literature to provide inspiration.

You'll discover that planning your feast is fun and the anticipation is exhilarating. Best yet, the afterglow will remain with you for a lifetime. Here is a husband's assessment of his experience:

"When we first started talking about going away—just the two of us—I got really excited. Sandy and I had never done anything like that before. And when we finally took off, it was like we were on our honeymoon again. For five blissful days, we left our problems and responsibilities at home and concentrated on the two of us. It was an experience I'll never forget and I highly recommend it to other couples."

Keep the Mystery in Sex

Liz and Parker, whom we discussed earlier, married when they were very young. Neither was very experienced sexually, but they consider that a plus in their relationship. As Parker put it:

"We learned on the job, so to speak. We taught each other and helped each other. And it was wonderful. Our honeymoon was truly an adventure as we explored and learned what it means to be a sexual being. And one of the things I learned is that there's mystery to sex. After twelve years of marriage and two children, I still don't fully understand it.

"Every time Liz and I have sex, there's an element of uncertainty. What will she want this time? What will turn her on? And there's also an element of discovery. We keep finding new ways to please each other. It amazes me that after twelve years I'm still learning, I'm still discovering, and I'm still as excited by sex with Liz as I ever was. That's why I say there's a mystery to sex. And I hope the mystery never goes away."

This is the challenge—to keep the mystery in sex. The alternative is for sex to become routine and even boring. Newlyweds sometimes look at us quizzically when we say this, replying, "Sex becomes routine or boring? You've gotta be kidding!" No, we're perfectly serious. A woman told us she believes that it's not possible for two people to find each other sexually exciting for more than five years. At the time, she had been married seven years. She was saying, in other words, that for at least two years she had found sex with her husband a dull affair at best.

She isn't alone. A considerable number of both men and women admit they have little interest in sex or that they are bored with sex with the same partner. Sometimes boredom leads to an affair. Sometimes it just leads to less and less meaningful sex. Rather than love play, sex becomes a periodic physical relief.

Sooner or later, *every* couple faces the challenge of keeping their sex life from becoming boring. So how do you respond to the challenge? How do you keep the mystery in sex? Let's look at some things that cause boredom, then at what can be done to prevent it.

Sex Suppressors

If you and your partner once enjoyed exciting sex but now find yourselves bored, one or more of the following suppressors may be the culprit. Assuming that you have no physical or emotional problems that affect your desire, your diminished sexual appetite may be due to the fact that you have placed a low priority on sex; you have a rigid schedule or an unchanging routine; or you neglect sexual turn-ons.

Putting a Low Priority on Sex When couples first begin a sexual relationship, they tend to have a problem keeping their hands off each other. Touching, hugging, kissing, fondling, and intercourse are a high priority in their lives. Eventually, the demands of everyday life force them to come to terms with the fact that life involves more than love play. In some cases, unfortunately, this translates into putting sex way down on their list of priorities.

Sex may be eclipsed on your priority list by a demanding career. Or by favorite TV programs. Or by a fascinating hobby. Or by children and household responsibilities. Sex becomes less important as these other things consume your time and energy. Perhaps you realize you still need sex but have lost sight of its importance for both your personal and couple well-being.

Adhering to a Rigid Schedule Sexual desire waxes and wanes in everyone. Nevertheless, we have known couples who insist on a rigid schedule for sex. It's OK to have a schedule. It may even be beneficial to have a schedule (we'll talk about it in Chapter 10). But a *rigid* schedule leaves you vulnerable to boredom.

If you decide, for instance, that you will have sex every Wednesday, Friday, and Sunday, what happens if you see an erotic movie on Saturday night? What happens if Wednesday is a bad day at the office and sexual desire has been wrung out of you? Sex can be more of a duty or even a nuisance rather than a form of love play when you keep it rigidly scheduled.

Following an Unchanging Routine "It's always the same," a wife complained. "I can tell you exactly what he's going to do and how long he's going to do it when we make love." For her, sex had become a highly scripted act to run through rather than a mystery to explore.

Sex that is totally predictable can easily become boring. One of the basic needs we all have is for new experiences, for novelty. Edith Wharton wrote of the distress of one her characters: "A haunting horror of doing the same thing every day at the same hour besieged his brain."[7] People do not function well generally when they have an unchanging routine. Nor do couples function well sexually when sex becomes a routine rather than a mystery.

Neglecting Sexual Turn-Ons A middle-aged man we know went through a period of grieving after his wife divorced him. Then he began to exercise, count his calories, and update his wardrobe. He became a different man. A year after the divorce he was healthier and more attractive than we had ever seen him. We have known a number of other people who, following a divorce or the death of a spouse, began to attend to their personal appearance and make themselves into more attractive people.

The question is, why didn't they do this for their partners? In some relationships, sex becomes boring or less appealing because one or both partners stop being sexually attractive. Or they neglect other kinds of sexual turn-ons—the kinds of things we discussed in the section on foreplay. Failure to use sexual turn-ons is a sure recipe for suppressing desire and nurturing boredom.

Mystery Cultivators

To maintain the mystery of sex, we suggest a five-part program:

1. Turn the suppressors on their heads.
2. Think about pleasure, not performance.
3. Focus on arousing your partner.
4. Use books and videos.
5. Keep it playful.

Turn the Suppressors on Their Heads The most obvious way to keep the mystery in sex is to avoid the suppressors—in fact, you should do the very opposite. Agree to keep sex and other love play a high priority in your relationship. If you have a schedule, don't be rigid about keeping it. In fact, deliberately break it at times. If you have a routine that is exciting to you, keep it up. But bring in something new from time to time. Make it a goal to find novel ways to please each other.

Finally, attend carefully to sexual turn-ons. Keep yourself sexually attractive, the way you would if you were in the market for a mate. Do the kinds of things that comprise good foreplay. Look for anything particular that is a sexual turn-on for your partner and then use it.

Think About Pleasure, Not Performance "How was I?" How often have you heard that line (if not from your partner, then in a book or movie)? Or how often have you spoken or even thought the same thing? It's a line that indicates a high concern for performance. Certainly, most of us want to perform well sexually. But it's more important to experience pleasure than to set a performance record.

If you think too much about performance, sex becomes a skill to master rather than a mystery to explore. And if you ever master it, you lose the mystery. So concentrate on pleasure. Think about enjoying the experience and not on rating it according to some performance standard.

Focus on Arousing Your Partner   This doesn't contradict what we just wrote. In fact, it is a delightful way to probe the mystery of sex while enhancing your own pleasure. When you focus on arousing your partner, you encounter mystery, because what works one time may not work as well the next. Every sexual encounter becomes a new opportunity to discover what maximizes your partner's sexual fulfillment.

At the same time, arousing your partner intensifies your own pleasure. As psychoanalyst Michael Balder wrote, there are four reasons why arousing your partner also turns you on.[8] First, it is a "natural human longing" to make one's partner happy. Second, being with someone who's aroused is exciting. Third, your partner's arousal is inherently affirming (so, yes, you are performing well). And, fourth, the arousal powerfully assures you that your partner is happy in this sexual experience.

Use Books and Videos   People sometimes think of information in books and other media as a way to solve mysteries. Changing weather patterns, for example, may be a mystery to you until you read a book that explains all the factors involved. In the case of sex, however, the books and videos available maintain rather than diminish the mystery of sex because they give you new ideas and new perspectives. They help you bring novelty into your sex life. And they remind you to keep sex as a high priority.

Available books range from the ancient (such as the *Kama Sutra*) to the recent (such as *The New Joy of Sex*). Rather than recommend specific books, however, we suggest you go to a bookstore and browse until you find something that appeals to you. Similarly, a number of videos are available, including some that are aimed specifically at showing you how to satisfy each other sexually. Again, check out what's there, read the description, and decide whether it's for you.

When you use these resources, keep in mind that just because it's in a book or on a video doesn't mean that it's right for you. Unless you're both comfortable with a particular practice, you shouldn't do it. The aim of using books and videos is not to test the limits of what you're willing to do, but to bring you together into the mystery of sex.

Keep It Playful Like Paula, Hank did not have a satisfying sexual relationship in his first marriage: "My first wife thought of sex as something you did as quickly as possible in the dark with your eyes closed." With Paula, on the other hand, Hank is discovering the mystery of sex:

> "I almost became sexless with my first wife. But with Paula, sex has become something wonderful. It's playful. Like one night, she wanted to put the condom on me. And she took a really long time doing it. She loves doing playful things like that, and so do I. You just never know what's next."

Being playful keeps the mystery in sex. You can never be sure what's next. It might be something like the husband who impulsively tickled his wife's feet as he came to bed. Or the wife who, after particularly satisfying sex, said, "Well, that's another chore I can scratch off my to-do list," then burst out laughing. Such playfulness helps keep sex a mystery that you never fully understand, never fully solve, but joyfully explore together.

Play for Keeps

We have suggested a couple of times that you consider writing a letter to your partner. When we conduct marriage enrichment weekends, we usually include writing and mailing love letters as one of the exercises. It's time now for your love letters.

Begin your letter with an affirmation of your partner. Then think about the materials in this chapter on foreplay. Tell your partner the kinds of things that he or she does that heighten your sexual desire. Follow this with a description of any love surprises you recall that were particularly meaningful to you. Tell how they made you feel.

Finally, think about those special sexual experiences you've had together. If you've had a love feast—a time that was especially romantic and sexually stimulating—tell your partner what you most loved about it. Or recall the most memorable sexual experience you've had together—the one that you found most exciting and satisfying, the one that best illustrates the wondrous mystery of sex. Write about it in your letter.

Close your letter with another affirmation of your partner. Then mail your letters (the suspense of waiting is part of the fun). After you receive and read them, talk about what you each have written and what you will do as a followup.

8

Creative Play

For six years, Lonnie and Dan reserved nearly every Friday evening for couple play. They had an established routine: a movie at a nearby theater, a mushroom and onion pizza at a neighborhood restaurant, then sex. It was a routine that Dan looked forward to, a welcome respite after a hectic week at work. He thought Lonnie felt the same—that is, until one Friday evening when she announced that they were in a rut and needed to try something different:

"I wasn't sure what she meant. 'But we always go to the movies and out for pizza on Fridays,' I reminded her. 'Yes,' she said, 'and we always go to the same movie theater and the same pizza parlor, and you give me that same look when we get home that asks me if we're going to have sex. Don't you ever want to do something different and more creative?'"

Actually, it hadn't occurred to him. He found their Friday evening routine comfortable and relaxing. But Lonnie's challenge caught his attention—maybe it was time for a change, although he did balk at the suggestion of "creative play." "I'm just not a creative person," he said. Lonnie reassured him that finding ways to play creatively was a shared task, not his sole responsibility. However, in the course of their efforts, Dan learned that he, like everyone else, has the ability to be creative in planning couple play.

When God Gave Out Creativity . . .

Creativity, we believe, is a gift that is given to all. God did not hand out creativity to a select few. If you doubt that—if, like Dan, you don't think of yourself as a creative person—you may need to rethink both the meaning of creativity and your own abilities.

Creativity: Ex Nihilo *Versus the Fosbury Flop*

In Judeo-Christian thought, God created the world *ex nihilo*.[1] That is, God created the world out of nothing. The universe was something totally new. If you think of creativity in these terms, as an act of bringing something totally new and beyond imagination into existence, then you're right about not being creative. Only God created *ex nihilo*; human creativity is on a different plane.

Consider the creativity of Dick Fosbury.[2] During his adolescence in the late 1950s and early 1960s, Fosbury was a high jumper. At the time he began competing, the standard method of high jumping was to get a running start, kick your lead leg out, and straddle the bar while keeping your face down.

Fosbury created a new method. He twisted around as he came to the bar and thrust himself up so that his head and shoulders cleared the bar first. With his back arched and his face looking into the sky, he "flopped" over the bar. The technique, which his coach initially tried to get him to abandon, became known as the *Fosbury flop*. It is now the standard method used by high jumpers throughout the world.

The Fosbury flop was a variation. People had high jumped before. They had done backflips before. Yet no one before Fosbury had combined a backflip with the high jump.

And that's the way we'd like for you to think of creativity in your couple play. We're not saying that you should create *ex nihilo*. Just think about doing some Fosbury flops. To be creative in your play simply means to plan and experience something that is new for you as a couple. It's something you *need* to do from time to time. And it's something you *can* do at any time.

Creativity: Elite Possession Versus a Universal Gift

If you think of creativity as Fosbury flops rather than *ex nihilo*, you can understand why we say that everyone has the capacity to be creative. Creativity isn't something that is confined to the Einsteins and Edisons of the world. It's also found in the Fosburys and in couples like Lonnie and Dan. As psychologist Robert Epstein has written, the "very good news" about creativity is that "you can boost your own creative output by a factor of 10 or more. Significant creativity is within everyone's reach—no exceptions. What's more, greater creativity breeds greater happiness."[3]

While he wasn't talking specifically about couple play, his statement applies: All couples can be creative in their play, and creativity leads to greater satisfaction in their relationship.

Creative play, as Lonnie and Dan learned, is a shared task, not something one of you does for the other. When you put your creative heads together, you gain important benefits:

- Working together gives you more than twice the creative power you have when each of you works separately (we have deduced this principle from years of working with couples and observing how wonderfully creative they can be when they work together).
- Because the creative process is a joint effort, you are both more invested and therefore more likely to enthusiastically try new ideas.

- As with anything you do together, being creative in your couple play is another bonding link in your chain of shared experiences and your unique couple history.

So what do you do when you put your creative heads together? How do you get started? A good place to begin is to ask yourselves the following four questions—questions that we'll explore in the remainder of this chapter:

1. Do we need a change?
2. Where can we get ideas?
3. How can we expand our play repertoire?
4. What can we do when resources are limited?

Do We Need a Change?

This first question is really a way of deciding whether it's time for you to be creative about your couple play. The axiom "If it ain't broke, don't fix it" applies here. If you're both perfectly delighted with your couple play, don't change it. We know couples, for example, who have played bridge weekly with the same group for the last twenty-five years. And they still love it. We know couples who vacation in the same place every year. After decades, they still joyfully anticipate relaxing in their cabin in the woods or cottage on the beach.

Of course, a weekly bridge night or a yearly vacation at a cabin retreat isn't the whole of their couple play. We know very few couples who are completely satisfied with the totality of their couple play, who feel no need for change of any kind. In our experience, even if you feel this way at the moment, sooner or later you will find yourself saying yes to the question of whether you need a change. When this moment comes, you will also need to ask a follow-up question: Which aspects of your couple play would you like to change?

Lonnie made it clear that she needed some variety in their Friday night play. Once she told Dan, their conversation proceeded like this:

> Dan: "I thought you liked going to movies at the mall."
> Lonnie: "I do. I just get tired of going to the same place week after week."
> Dan: "Well, it's close."
> Lonnie: "We don't always have to go someplace close, do we?"
> Dan: "Of course not. Let's see what's showing at some of the other theaters."

That night, they chose a different theater and ate at a different restaurant (they decided on seafood). It felt like an adventure, like "a minivacation," as Lonnie put it. Note that they didn't create something totally new. They did a Fosbury flop. They changed the way they went to the movies and had dinner on Friday. They also decided that, at least once a month, they'd go to the symphony or see a stage play instead of a movie.

Where Can We Get Ideas?

Return to your play profiles. Think about the six categories: social play, cultural play, humor, games, physical play, and love play. Review the kinds of activities that fall into each. In the "Play for Keeps" exercise in Chapter 3, we asked you to take the top two categories for both of you and expand the list of activities in each. Now take the remaining categories and do the same.

Read the entertainment sections of local newspapers for ideas about cultural play. Look at outdoor magazines for various kinds of physical play. Search the library and the Internet and you'll find numerous ideas for humor, games, and love play. Talk with other couples about how they play. Read the list of play activities in the last chapter of this book. And as you jot down various ideas, consider how you might vary them to suit your own situation and your particular tastes and needs. In other words, be creative.

For example, Zack and Rachel have a nine-month-old baby girl, Andi. They are runners. They ran together until Rachel became pregnant. Zack ran alone for most of Rachel's pregnancy. After Andi's birth, they began running separately; one ran while the other stayed home with the baby. One day Zack saw a woman running while pushing a three-wheeled jogging stroller, and he decided to surprise Rachel with one for her birthday. Now they are running together as a family. Rachel finds it exhilarating:

> "I've never liked running alone. And Zack and I are so busy that I hated to take that much time apart. Now we can exercise and still be together. It's an important time for us to chat and feel really connected with each other. And Andi loves it, too."

Similarly, Lonnie and Dan decided to engage in more physical play. Dan told us that they had decided that too much of their fun time featured "side-by-side" activities. "We were either sitting silently in a movie or in front of the TV," he said. "We really weren't interacting very much when we were together." But it was a creative response to a "side-by-side" activity that inspired a change in their activities.

One night after they had watched an old Fred Astaire and Ginger Rogers movie on video, Lonnie confessed to Dan: "You know what I've always wanted to try? Ballroom dancing." But this was a whopper of a challenge: Lonnie had little experience with dancing and Dan had none at all. The biggest thing they had going for them was their admiration for Fred and Ginger and a yearning to dance like them—at least to a limited degree.

Lonnie suggested that they take a class together. Although the only class they could find was offered at an inconvenient time, Lonnie was not ready to give up on the idea. She located and purchased a video with detailed instructions on ballroom dancing, and they started practicing at home:

> "We had to keep rewinding and replaying segments of the tape before we could get it right. Dan doesn't have a great sense of rhythm, and I'm pretty clumsy. We spent half of our time laughing at our mistakes—any resemblance to Ginger and Fred was purely coincidental. But we stayed with it. And while we're not great, we feel comfortable going out on the dance floor anywhere. We love it!"

Both Zack and Rachel and Lonnie and Dan got their ideas by watching others. This may be one of your better sources. Keep your eyes open. Observe other people at play. Think about yourselves doing the same things. You'll find that there's more than a lifetime of possibilities for your couple play.

How Can We Expand Our Play Repertoire?

There's an old story about a man who played the cello, but he only played the same note—over and over again. When a friend asked him why, he replied, "Some people are still searching, but I've found it—the perfect note." He may have been satisfied, but a person with a repertoire of only one note is impoverished. The world of music is too extensive and rich to be satisfied with hearing only a minute fraction of it.

The same kind of thing can happen in the world of couple play. There are many options available to you. And you impoverish yourselves when you limit your repertoire to one or two.

All couples tend to get into ruts. Perhaps, like Lonnie and Dan, you think of your Friday-night routine as a warm, fuzzy blanket at the end of a hectic work week. Or maybe you feel that you don't have the time to think of new things to do. Or you've slipped into a funk of sameness and can't seem to pull yourself out. We urge you to fight these impulses and expand your play repertoires. That is, expand the number of things you enjoy doing together.

Experiment

So how do you expand your repertoire? The answer is simple: experiment. You might find it fun to give some of the pastimes you enjoyed earlier in your life together another chance. For example, when we were first married, we kept a large jigsaw puzzle on the coffee table and worked on it whenever the mood struck us. The practice stopped, however, when our first child became a toddler and delighted in scattering the pieces as far as he could around the room. Puzzles and Jon, we discovered, couldn't coexist in the same space. Recently, after many years, we have resumed the practice and find ourselves once again enjoying the challenge of fitting together a thousand or more puzzle pieces into a beautiful picture.

Or you might want to experiment with something that's new, at least for the two of you as a couple. It can be something that both of you have done before but not together, or something that one of you but not the other has done, or something that neither of you has ever done.

Consider Zack and Rachel, whom you met earlier in this chapter. Before their daughter was born, both of them competed in local and regional racing events. For the time being, however, Andi has changed all that. But they've discovered new outlets for their competitive urges—chess and gin rummy. As they thought about ways to bring more play into their relationship, they read about a couple who had a weekly Scrabble match. Rachel wasn't sure it would work for them:

"I didn't want to get into too much competition with Zack. Before I had Andi, we frequently competed against each other. When we ran together, one of us might try to push for a little extra mileage or a little faster pace, and we would sprint the last part of the run to see who would finish first.

"Our rivalry never got out of hand, but it came close at times. Now that Andi accompanies us on our runs, we no longer compete; we just enjoy the run and the chance to be together. So even though I was hesitant at first, I agreed to a weekly board game with Dan."

They tried a number of different games. The trick was to find ones that were sufficiently engaging without rousing their competitive spirits too intensely. They quickly abandoned a few possibilities when they found themselves engaged in a fierce battle rather than a friendly game. Eventually they settled on chess and an occasional game of gin rummy. They're delighted with the result:

"Neither of us had played these kind of games since we were adolescents. It's really fun getting back into them. And the neat thing is that they're right there waiting for us whenever we're ready. In fact, we always seem to have a game of chess in progress. Often after Andi is in bed, we hover over the board for an hour or so. It's a lot of fun, and we're both getting pretty good at it."

You can also experiment with activities neither of you has tried before. And when we say "experiment," we mean both trying something new and doing it in a way that works for you. It needn't be something daring and exotic, like a float trip down the Amazon or an afternoon of skydiving. A friend once urged us to try skydiving because it "gives you the biggest adrenaline rush you'll ever experience." We took his word for it. We applaud those of you who are more daring and greater risk-takers than we are, but our own foray into something we had never done before was less spectacular. Still, it has been highly rewarding to try new things.

We both enjoy reading and have friends who are also avid readers. We were talking about our mutual interest one evening when one of our friends suggested we start a book group. How does a book group function? None of us had ever been part of such a group. But we determined not to let our lack of experience deter us. We decided to start the group and work out the procedures along the way. And that's what we did. Four other couples joined us, and we have met monthly for nearly fifteen years.

Having no idea how book groups typically function (and not particularly concerned about being typical), we developed the following guidelines, which work for us:

- We meet in our homes on a rotating basis. Dates are not fixed but are discussed and set in advance for three to four months.
- The couple hosting the meeting selects and purchases the book and distributes it to the other couples at the prior month's meeting. Sometimes an assignment will be given along with the book—some questions or issues raised by the book to think about as we read.
- Any kind of book is acceptable—fiction or nonfiction. We have read classic as well as contemporary novels, poetry, biography, theology, psychology, and various other kinds of nonfiction. We have occasionally had an author meet with us to discuss his or her work.
- The couple hosting the meeting provides dinner for the group. Generally, the dinner includes items mentioned in the book or reflects in some way the theme of the book.
- Discussion of the book itself does not occur during dinner. Rather, dinner is a time for catching up with each other's lives and discussing current events.
- How to structure the after-dinner discussion of the book is left to the discretion of the hosts. They may have specific topics to talk about or simply throw open the discussion to the group.

The book group was an experiment for all of us. It has proven to be such a successful experiment that our pleasure in it shows no sign of abating after more than a decade.

Plan for the Future

We have worked with numerous engaged couples and newlyweds. Most, we have found, don't think of couple play as an important issue that will face them in the future. But it will. So we remind them that:

- Your tastes will change over the years, which means that you won't want to do indefinitely some of the things you do now.
- Your resources will vary over the years, which means that you may not have the time or money to do some of the things you now enjoy.
- Because you anticipate a future together, you need to plan for your couple play just as you plan for other important matters like children and a home.

The way to plan for the future is to expand your repertoire of couple play. We recommend that on a regular basis—perhaps weekly or monthly—you do something together that you each define as play and that you have never done together. You can work as a team to plan the activities, or you can take turns making plans.

Don't exclude activities just because you don't find them initially appealing. You might discover a winner or two that will become lifelong pursuits. Or you might decide to put others on the back burner as possible activities for the future. Many couples, for example, arrive at the empty-nest phase of life and find themselves able to pursue in earnest an interest that was too demanding during the child-rearing years.

The point is, as you regularly try something new you will find yourselves building a repertoire of activities that you enjoy. They are there standing in the wings when you need them. And you *will* need them. They are going to make your future together as vibrant as your present.

What Can We Do When Resources Are Limited?

If you have a good deal of discretionary time and unlimited financial resources, you obviously have more options available to you for couple play. It may be relatively easy for you to be creative. However, if you're like the majority of people, you will encounter periods of your life when both time and money are limited.

That describes us perfectly. At various points in our marriage we have had too little money to travel or to indulge in other kinds of play. At other times, we've had enough money to do what we wanted but not enough time. How can you be creative when you face such limits?

When Time Is Limited

You may not have the time for many activities you desire, such as an extended vacation, traveling to Tahiti, weekly golf or tennis games, a three-day love feast, daily long walks, or season tickets for the symphony. Some activities may have to be put into your repertoire of future couple play. Lonnie and Dan have a dream of spending four weeks bicycling in Europe. "We can afford it," she notes, "but we just can't get four weeks off from work." So they've put it in their repertoire for the future.

On the other hand, there are ways you can be creative even when your schedule seems to preclude a desired form of couple play. First, you can shorten an activity, and, second, you can try it at an unconventional time.

Shorten a Play Activity There's no reason to forgo something you want to do simply because you don't think you have the required amount of time. You can usually adjust the time needed to the time you have available. Here are some ways that couples have shortened their play activities rather than abandoning them.

- "We wanted to take a two-week trip to the mountains but just couldn't take the time, so we settled for a week instead."
- "We love to get out for eighteen holes of golf, but for duffers like us that's a full day. So when we can't take the time, we settle for nine holes or a three-par course."
- "A three-day love feast is impossible for us right now; for now we can only manage a day."
- "We set up our game of Monopoly, play as long as we can, leave it set up, and finish the game at another time."
- "We sometimes dance at home instead of taking the time to go out somewhere."
- "We booked a prepackaged vacation instead of using a lot of time to plan and make our own arrangements."
- "We never watch a TV program when it's aired. We tape what we want and watch it later so we can fast forward through the commercials. It's amazing how much less time we spend in front of the television set."

Try an Unconventional Time If couples hold back from an activity because they don't have enough time, they also often hesitate because they can't do it at what they regard as the "right" time. That is, the time when they *usually* do something. For example, we advised a man and woman who were struggling with their sexual relationship. The wife worked at a department store where her schedule varied from day to day. Her husband worked from noon until late evening. By the time he got home, he was usually too tired for sex. "I go to bed too many nights feeling sexually frustrated," she complained.

Looking at their schedules, we pointed out something that somehow hadn't occurred to them: "You have a number of mornings when you're both home. Why don't you have sex then?" However, this was an unconventional time for them. They thought of sex as something they did only at night after they went to bed. What a revelation! They discovered that the "right" time for sex is any time.

Similarly, a couple told us about their efforts to develop a friendship with another couple:

"We met them when our sons played on the same soccer team, and we really liked them. We agreed that we'd go out to dinner together and tried for a couple weeks to come up with a time. But every night we had open they had something, and any night they chose we had something. Then we realized that we all worked fairly close to each other downtown. Why not get together for lunch instead of dinner? And that's what we've done."

Time, whether you're thinking of the necessary amount of time or the "right" time, is no barrier to those who are creative in their couple play.

When Money Is Limited

We love to watch children play. They can take pots and pans, cardboard boxes, dirt, and a host of other things readily available and use them to play. For them, the lack of money doesn't mean they can't play.

Playing with pots and pans, no doubt, holds little appeal for you. But you can still learn from the kids. For instance, how about trying one of their favorite kinds of cost-free play: make-believe? In make-believe, you can pretend for at least a little while to be a different person. Be a movie star, a sophisticated lover, a supremely self-confident individual, or anyone else you admire.

If you really want to enrich your relationship while you play, pretend to be a better person. For example, if you tend not to articulate your appreciation, pretend to be a person who is quick to point out all the good things about your partner and to express appreciation for every loving act. This kind of pretending can have long-term benefits, because you'll find yourself becoming more like the person you are pretending to be.

There are numerous other ways to play that are free or relatively inexpensive. When we were at a point in our lives where we had limited resources but rather expensive tastes, we had dreams for our home that we couldn't afford. What we *could* afford, however, was to walk through model homes, observe the decorating schemes, and make mental notes for what we wanted to do in the future.

Here are some other activities that work for couples with limited resources (as well as for those not limited):

- Go for a picnic in the park.
- Invite some couples over for a potluck dinner.
- Identify and take advantage of the events, activities, and resources that are free in your community (don't forget to check the local library).
- Use the track at a nearby school to walk, jog, or run.
- Invite the neighbors over to share a bottle of wine.
- Rent some movies and have your own film festival, complete with popcorn and drinks.
- If you play a musical instrument or sing, volunteer to perform at an extended-care facility.

Don't underestimate the value of such low-cost activities. A man told us that one of the most pleasurable experiences he had with his wife occurred on a day they explored a section of the Kentucky countryside in the late fall: "We just decided to see what we could see."

They strolled around a number of small towns, were awed by the fall colors, and enjoyed some fascinating chats with local residents. "And all it cost us was the price of the gas and lunch," he recalled. Memorable experiences come in many different forms. And some of them require minimal time and money.

Play for Keeps

We listed four questions for you to use in stimulating your creative juices. Here's a fifth: How can we do this differently? Select two or three of your favorite activities, and see how many different ways you can come up with to engage in them.

For instance, if one of your favorite forms of couple play is eating out, how could you vary it? How about trying a different ethnic food every month? Or going to one restaurant for the main course and another for the dessert? Why not ask the chef to fix an entree for you in a special way?

How about starting a "dining-out club" with a number of couples? Perhaps your group could scout out new and interesting restaurants, some of which might even involve travel. Dining out is one of our high-priority activities. We have had memorable meals in small towns, ranging from Fort Bragg, California, to Lake George, New York. And we have one regret. At a restaurant in Austin, Texas, the chef offered a "surprise" meal. He selected everything from the appetizer to the dessert to the wine. At the time, we weren't sufficiently adventurous to take advantage of the offer. We've regretted it ever since. The point is, a dining club can identify such possibilities within a reasonable area and set you off on a joint gastronomic adventure.

After you've identified a number of alternative ways of engaging in your favorite activities, try some of them. You may want to return to your usual pattern, but you also may discover that your creative efforts yield some "keepers," some new ways of engaging in couple play that you'll want to continue.

9

Play Niches in Ordinary Time

When asked why there wasn't more play in their lives, the man responded with a hint of sarcasm: "We're not kids. We have a lot of responsibilities. We come home from work and there's still more work to do. Our parents taught us to 'work before play,' and I have to tell you there isn't much time in our lives for play right now."

A lot of us have been nurtured on the adage "Work before play." We grew up thinking of this as not merely a piece of advice, but a moral principle. We learned to think of play as something we earned by finishing our work. We came to believe that the main value of play was to prepare us to plunge eagerly back into work.

On the positive side, this principle produces responsible adults. It also reflects sound psychology: play is a way to reward yourself for working, thereby reinforcing your will to work. On the negative side, the adage turns some people, like the man we quoted, into overly responsible workaholics. It also suggests that work and play are opposing activities. This obscures two important facts: first, you can often mix play with work; and second, you can find numerous play opportunities in what we call *ordinary time*—the time when you are engaged in routine activities. Both facts reinforce the point that opportunities for couple play abound.

Opportunities Are Everywhere

Think about the examples of silliness we gave in Chapter 6. The kind of situations in which they occurred are instructive: eating dinner, walking along a sidewalk, and sitting in the living room. They illustrate that opportunities for couple play are everywhere. As a professor of leisure studies puts it, walking along a sidewalk isn't a form of play. But if one notices the cracks in the sidewalk, "then begins to measure one's stride by those cracks, then tries to avoid stepping on those cracks—well, that's play."[1]

What's needed, then, is not a designated time, a particular place, or special resources, but rather a playful state of mind—a readiness to engage in play and an alertness to the many opportunities you face every day. One couple, for example, told us how they became playful in their affirmations of love:

> "Early in our marriage, when one of us would say to the other 'I love you,' the response would be 'I love you more.' Then the first would say, 'I love you even more than that.' And off we'd go, each trying to top the other. We don't do that anymore. But we still try to outdo each other in our claims of love, and we always end up laughing about it."

The opportunities are limitless. We recommend six actions that will help you take advantage of those opportunities and increase the number of your play niches in ordinary time:

1. Make your home a play reminder.
2. Combine individual chores with couple play.
3. Add play to mundane activities.

4. Turn simple pleasures into special moments.
5. Make your play decisions playful.
6. Fill small chunks of time with intimacy games.

Make Your Home a Play Reminder

Think about the homes you have visited. When you enter a home, it creates a mood in you. You may be immediately chilled by the fact that it is bare-boned housing, used for little other than sleeping and eating. Or that it is an immaculate shrine in which you need to be careful about touching anything. Or that it is a warm and inviting place that makes you feel welcome and at ease.

In other words, the way you decorate and maintain your home can create many moods—not just among those who visit, but also in you. So why not make your home a play reminder? If your home breeds a playful state of mind, you will be more alert for play opportunities wherever you are.

The Formula

Social psychologists have long recognized that mood affects behavior in important ways. For example, if you're feeling down, your thinking will generally be more negative. You'll be more apt to see the dark side of things. You may be less likely to help someone in need. By contrast, if you are in a good mood, you will see the world in a more positive light and be more likely to help others.[2] It's a reasonable conclusion, therefore, to suggest that a playful mood will enable you to recognize and take advantage of the many opportunities for play you encounter in ordinary time.

Of course, a playful home won't automatically create a playful mood. If you've just been fired, coming home to a playfully decorated house won't transform you from a depressed and angry worker into a playmate for your partner. Or if you and your partner are having an argument, the fact that it's taking place in your playful home won't quell your disagreement and turn you back into a pair of love-birds. Other things being equal, however, living in a playful home will create a playful mood and make you more sensitive and receptive to play opportunities.

Travel has increased our awareness of how important the atmosphere of a place is to our state of mind. A couple of years ago, for example, we stayed in a honeymoon suite because it was the only room left in a charming bed-and-breakfast. We were a long way from our honeymoon, but the suite created a romantic atmosphere. And we loved it! In contrast, we have also made reservations at highly touted hotels only to find ourselves in dingy, ill-kept rooms that created instant gloom and depressed any romantic thought.

So here's the formula: atmosphere will create the mood, which leads to the behavior. The atmosphere is a playful home. The mood is a playful state of mind. The behavior is more couple play in ordinary time.

The Playful Home

How, then, do you make your home a playful one? A basic rule, following the rule for all couple play, is that it must be playful for both of you. It isn't playful to have a sports theme run throughout the house unless you're both passionate about sports. It isn't playful to have a decorating style that makes you feel giddy if it makes your partner feel queasy.

There is, therefore, no single formula for creating a playful home. You have to do what works for you. Here are some of the things you can consider, based on what other couples have done:

- Use bright, vivid paint or wallpaper on your walls—
  something that makes you both feel cheerful.

- Turn one room into a rec room (a play room for adults) and use it to pursue hobbies, play games, and work out together.
- Surround yourselves with pictures and other artifacts that bring smiles to your faces.
- Place some playful conversation pieces around that rouse curiosity and amuse your visitors.
- Display mementoes of particularly enjoyable times in places where you see them frequently.
- Use an occasional offbeat piece of furniture to highlight a room.
- Add quirky touches to your decor such as a play spider on a potted plant, a large mirror above the bed, a doorknob shaped like an extended hand, and so on.
- Have different themes for different rooms, themes that reflect your interests or your experiences.

These may not work for you, but you get the idea. Think of your home as a mood-shaper. And then get started (a few steps at a time) in creating the atmosphere you desire.

One thing that we do is to place mementos we have collected in our travels around the house. These serve as a constant reminder of the fun we've had together. For instance, Bob collects moose in all shapes and sizes. They range from delicate porcelain to stuffed figures, from a quarter of an inch to six feet tall, and from fine art to homespun crafts. He chose moose as collectibles because they're "clumsy and horny"—two adjectives he uses to describe himself. Maybe that's why they never fail to bring a smile to us, as well as to those who visit our home.

One moose gets particular attention. It is a gift from a former Middle Eastern student who admired the collection. He brought it back after a visit to his native country. It's actually a giraffe. "This was the closest thing I could find to a moose," he explained.

Combine Individual Chores with Couple Play

We share something in common with a lot of other couples we know: Jeanette is a careful shopper who enjoys looking until she finds just what she wants; Bob suffers from a relentless aversion to department stores. As a result, we've gone through three phases in the shopping chore. The first phase was going together, with Jeanette doing her thing and Bob trudging along behind her. It didn't work well; Jeanette tired of his hovering behind her with that pained look on his face.

So in the second phase, shopping became her individual chore while Bob stayed home and worked (or so he said). This made shopping a lot more pleasant for Jeanette but left us both dissatisfied. Like most couples, there are too many demands in our lives that force us to go our separate ways, so we cherish the time we have together. We have found that the more things we do as a couple, the stronger our bond and the deeper our intimacy.

This led us to the third phase. How could we combine our individual chores with a time of couple play? We decided that, whenever possible, we'd drive together to the shopping center. And while Jeanette shops, Bob finds a table and a cup of coffee and uses the time to get caught up on his reading. After Jeanette has finished, we have dinner and drive home together. This way we enjoy some of the time together—time that we would otherwise spend separately.

One way to combine couple play with individual chores, then, is to find ways to do some chores together. For example, if she typically cleans the house while he takes care of the yard, why not do these chores together? You can enjoy each other while doing them. You'll have some extra time together and the chores will be less onerous.

Even if you can't do individual chores together on a regular basis, you may be able to do so on occasion. Martha and Donald are always up for couple play. However, Martha does a lot of baking and, at least the way she does it, it's clearly an individual chore. But on one occasion she invited Donald to help her. She had agreed to bake five varieties of cookies for a Christmas bake sale at her daughter's school and asked Don for some help. As it turned out, Don proved a disaster in the kitchen. He dusted himself and the kitchen counter with flour, spilled chocolate chips all over the floor, and mistakenly substituted chili powder for cinnamon. But his ineptness had the makings of a legend. "To this day," Martha says, "we laugh about Don's 'hot cookies.' "

On another occasion, Donald was digging up an old stump in the backyard while Martha did the laundry. It was a hot summer day, as Donald tells it:

> "I was tired and sweaty and needed a drink. Normally, I'd just take a break and go into the house. Instead, I got the urge to do something different. So I called Marty on my cell phone. When she answered, I said, 'Marty, I need you to come out here and give me a kiss.' She was silent for a moment; it startled her to hear my voice on the telephone. 'Where are you?' she finally asked. I told her I was still in the backyard. 'And while you're at it,' I said, 'could you bring me a pitcher of ice water?'
>
> "She came out with the water and a grin. We both took a break from our work and talked about what we were doing. A little while later after she'd gone back into the house, my cell phone rang. It was her. 'I forgot the kiss,' she said. 'Can I give it to you when you come in?' I told her she could give me that and anything else she had in mind."

Add Play to Mundane Activities

There's a story about an older wife advising a newly married woman about housework: It won't get you down if you decide ahead of time that you're never going to get finished. Whenever you look around and think you've done a good job, just remember that even while you're congratulating yourself, the sheets are wrinkling, the dust is settling on the furniture, and the kitchen is waiting for you to fix the next meal.

That's one view of housework—a dreary task that never ends but must be done. A different view is set forth by author Kathleen Norris. She asks whether an individual must "choose between a life of the mind and a life of repetitive, burdensome work."[3] She answers the question by arguing that routine household tasks are a form of love and service, not a necessary nuisance that interrupts the good things of life. Learning such things as how to bake bread, she writes, made her "a better-grounded person, more in touch with the real world, and allowed me to cast off the aimless and overly cerebral young woman that I had become."[4]

Clearly, you can view mundane activities like housework in very different ways—as anything from routine tasks of drudgery to acts of loving service. We recommend the latter. It helps if you keep in mind that they are all tasks that need to be done and that by doing them you are making life a little better and easier for someone else. And if you add couple play to these mundane activities, it will be the icing on the cake.

Here are some ways that couples incorporate play into their everyday chores:

Washing and drying clothes at the laundromat can be an exercise in boredom even if you think of it as an act of loving service. One couple who does this chore together spends the time "getting to know others who are there; we end with a contest to see who can fold the most clothes in five minutes."

Driving consumes a good deal of time. You can have many trips of thirty minutes or longer, even for non-work purposes. Here is how Martha and Donald handle them:

"We make up different kinds of games to while away the time. Like one evening we were driving home from the theater and saw this beautiful harvest moon. We started thinking of all the songs with 'moon' in them and sang as many of them as we remembered. Another time we were talking about my job as an English teacher. I was in the midst of teaching my students about metaphors and similes. So we looked around as we drove, picked out objects like clouds in the sky or unusually shaped buildings, and came up with as many metaphors and similes as we could."

Coming home or *meeting* after being apart can be an important bonding experience. We were at a party when a friend arrived late. His girlfriend had come earlier, knowing that business would detain him. He greeted various people, nodded at his girlfriend, then began a conversation with another guest. They are no longer a couple. In contrast, a woman with a strong, vibrant marriage tells how she and her husband never take reunions for granted: "When we come home, or when we meet someplace, we always hug and kiss. I hope we never get to the point where seeing each other is a ho-hum thing for either of us."

Cooking dinner is a task shared by many couples. For some it is just another chore to get through. For others, it becomes a time of couple play. Here's what Simon told us:

"Allison and I love cooking dinner together. We always use it as a time to talk about what's happened during the day. It's a great opportunity for us to reconnect after being apart all day. We also like to experiment. We'll be fixing something and decide to see what it would taste like if we added a particular spice or herb. Once in a while we pretend we're gourmet cooks, get out our international cookbook, and try something really exotic."

Eating dinner, whether at home or at a restaurant, can be a perfunctory routine or a playful bonding time. We grew up with very different experiences. At Bob's house, meals were served and eaten quickly and silently. Dinner was something that had to be done before getting on with more important or interesting matters. At Jeanette's house, dinner was a leisurely time of food and conversation. You can do it either way, but we recommend the latter.

You won't want to turn every mundane activity into play, of course. Sometimes while driving you may prefer a serious conversation. Or music. Or quiet. The point is not to replace all the mundane with play, but to realize the possibilities you have for turning mundane activities into acts of loving service and times of couple play.

Turn Simple Pleasures into Special Moments

Let's go back to dinner. Eating a well-prepared dinner is one of the pleasures of life. It becomes even more enjoyable when accompanied by lively conversation. And it becomes a special moment when couple play turns it into a memorable event. Donald recalls one such meal:

> "It was a time when our budget was tight. We were on our way to a relative's wedding and planned to stay overnight at this hotel. It was late when we arrived. We were tired, so we decided to eat at the hotel. Its restaurant turned out to have a very pricey and upscale menu. When I looked at the menu, I was stunned by the prices. Marty whispered: 'Should we just leave?' I said no and declared, 'Damn the prices, full speed ahead!' From that point on, we had fun. We laughed about our ignorance about some of the utensils on our table, joked about acting like a rich couple, speculated about the occupations and interests of other customers, and thoroughly enjoyed one of the best—and most expensive—meals we have ever had. It was truly a night to remember."

The meal could have been a nightmare of anxiously trying to keep the cost down. Instead, couple play turned it into a special moment.

As you add play to your simple pleasures, you create a wealth of special moments. Consider music. If you're like us, you often have music playing around the house. It's another way to create a playful home. But do more than listen. Take a break from your chores and sing or dance together. Let the simple pleasure of music turn into a time of couple play. Let the music become, in Shakespeare's words, the "food of love."[5]

You don't have to sing well to enjoy it or to have it become a special moment. Jamie recalls such a moment when her husband, Rex, broke into song:

> "Rex loves music, but he can barely carry a tune. We were listening to the radio when Joe Cocker started singing one of Rex's favorites, 'You Are So Beautiful.' Rex turned to me, took my hand, and began to sing along. I was touched by the fact that he was emphasizing the word *you* and looking at me as he sang. And I got tickled by his attempt to imitate Joe Cocker's voice. Before the song ended, we were both in stitches. I had tears in my eyes, partly from laughing and partly from being moved by Rex's sincere expression of love. It was wonderful."

Dancing can also turn the pleasure of music into a special moment. Dancing, as Rebecca Abrams wrote, is "a form of physical play that combines the joy of making noise with the profound pleasure of uninhibited self-expression."[6] Rex and Jamie met at a dancing class. They like to go out dancing and often engage in spur-of-the-moment dancing at home. One such occasion turned a frustrating time into a special moment:

> "Rex was doing our taxes. It's always a frustrating job for him. He gets upset over how much we have to pay. I was finishing up the dishes, and, as usual, we had music playing. I could see that Rex was agitated. 'Hey,' I said to him, 'the music's on. Let's dance a while. You can finish that stuff later.' He mumbled something about wanting to get it over with, but he tossed his pencil down and we began to dance.

"I don't remember what music was playing, but it reminded me of one of those sensual Arabian dances. So I started swaying my body around. I guess it was erotic. Rex got that look on his face and pretty soon we were headed for the bedroom. When he went back to the taxes, he was humming."

Make Your Play Decisions Playful

Decisions about couple play are responses to such questions as "Which movie shall we see?" "Where shall we eat dinner?" "Where should we spend our vacation this year?" "How would you like to celebrate our anniversary?" And so on. For many couples, the decision-making process can be both labored and irritating. A labored process might go like this:

"Where would you like to eat dinner tonight?"

"I don't know. Do you have any preference?"

"No. Do you?"

"No. I'm up for whatever you are."

"I'm not sure what I want."

"Me neither. Are you sure there's nothing that appeals to you?"

Recognize this conversation? When we describe this labored process with couples, we get a lot of knowing and sheepish grins. And we doubt that you're very different. One couple told us they have discovered that often the time it takes to make a decision about where to go or what to do takes as long as the activity itself.

The process can become irritating if those involved have opposing desires. For a number of years, we regularly went to the movies with another couple. Usually we had no problem deciding what to see. On one occasion, however, the process faltered. After a short discussion, three of us agreed we wanted to see a particular movie, but the fourth person wanted to see a different one. He was adamant. The conversation between the man and his wife went something like this:

M: "I've been looking forward to seeing this movie all week."

W: "But the rest of us don't want to see it."

M: "Well, I don't want to see yours either."

W: "Look, let's go see the one we want tonight, and we'll all go with you to see yours next week."

M: "I want to see it tonight. Why can't we ever do what I want?"

Although he finally agreed to see the movie the three of us preferred, the expression on his face hovered somewhere between surliness and anger. Needless to say, it wasn't one of the more enjoyable evenings we've had.

When making a decision about play is labored or frustrating, it detracts from the enjoyment. Why not turn the decision-making process itself into a form of play? A couple told us how they make a game out of it. If, for instance, they want to go out to eat, they each take five slips of paper and write down the name of a different restaurant on each slip. They put all the slips into a hat, then draw them out one by one. As they do, they see which restaurants they have chosen as possibilities. The one they go to that evening is the last one they pull out.

Another way to turn decision making into play is to take turns being responsible for the decision. Use the following rules:

- Decide which decisions you will include (where to eat, what movie to see, where to go on vacation, what new form of play you'll try this month).
- Decide whether you will alternate within categories ("I chose the movie last time; it's your turn tonight") or across categories ("I chose the movie last week; it's your turn to choose where we'll eat tonight").
- Flip a coin to see who begins.
- No sour grapes permitted. Go with the choice and enjoy it even if it wasn't your preference.

Fill Small Chunks of Time with Intimacy Games

You will find yourselves regularly having small chunks of time with no play activities planned. These chunks include those times when you are waiting—in a long line, for a table in a restaurant, in a traffic jam, or at the airport. What can you do with these small chunks of time?

You can, of course, get frustrated or angry. Or you can relax and meditate. Or you can engage in play that will make the time enjoyable rather than irritating. We suggest two kinds of intimacy games that are well suited to filling small chunks of time: word play and sharing dreams and fantasies.

Word Play

Again, we learn from children. Some of the word play we have observed among children that you also might enjoy includes:

- Hangman
- Making up different words to well-known songs
- Creating acronyms (for example, JOKER stands for "Jeff open-mouth kisses every redhead"—an adult version to be sure, but you get the idea)
- Making up short rhymes about each other (for example, variations of "Roses are red, violets are blue")
- Thinking of as many words that begin with the same letter of the alphabet as you can in thirty seconds, then seeing who can use the most of them in a sentence

An adult word game dating back hundreds of years involves taking a group of rhyming words and seeing who can make the best poem out of them. For instance, use the words *ham, ma'am, dam,* and *ram* to make a four-line poem. If you're ambitious, you can take six or more words. Or you can try two sets of rhyming words, with the lines of your poem alternating between them: *ham, play, ma'am, day.*

Another enjoyable form of adult word play is to see how many steps it will take you to transform one word into another by changing one letter at a time. Each change must result in a known word. For instance, how many steps would it take you to change *hack* into *hold*? You could do it this way: *hack - hock - honk - hone - hole - hold.* Can you do it in fewer steps? An easy way to come up with words to use is to think of opposing words. Try changing such pairs as *give* into *take, dawn* into *dusk,* or, if you prefer greater challenges, opposing words of five or more letters such as *white* into *black.*

You can also work crossword puzzles together. Or be creative and make up your own form of word play. And if any of this sounds inane or trivial, we have a question and a reminder for you. The question is, would you prefer to sit and stew in frustration or boredom? The reminder is that word play is a way of connecting with your partner, of having fun together. That's why we call it an intimacy game.

Sharing Dreams and Fantasies

Who are you as a couple? What kind of relationship do you have? Such questions are answered, in part, by your past experiences together. You have a unique history as a couple that has fashioned your relationship. Another part of the answer, however, involves the dreams and fantasies you share. If your relationship is being pushed in a particular direction by your past experiences, it is also being pulled in a particular direction by your dreams and fantasies.

What are your dreams and fantasies? If it were possible to tabulate the contents of every intimate conversation, we suspect that this kind of sharing would represent a very small fraction. That's unfortunate. You need to share your dreams and fantasies with each other. It doesn't matter if some of them are impractical or beyond your grasp. Sharing them deepens your understanding of each other and gives shape to your changing relationship.

So what would you like to do, individually and as a couple? To become? To achieve? More concretely, how would you respond to the following?

- Your notions of an ideal family life
- Where you want to go career-wise
- What you would do with the money if you won the lottery
- What an ideal sex life would look like for you
- Your hopes for your home, including location, furnishings, landscaping
- How you'd like to grow as a person
- Places you want to visit
- Skills you'd like to develop
- Experiences that would thrill you
- The kind of relationship you'd like to have ten years from now

When you're sharing thoughts about such matters—which you can fit into those small chunks of time—don't worry about whether your desires could or will actually be fulfilled. Remember, they're dreams and fantasies. They're both fun and revealing to talk about. And they give direction to your relationship. Thus, when a woman asked a man she was dating how he'd use the money if he won the lottery, his first response was: "I'm not going to win. I don't even buy tickets."

"That's not the point," she said. "Just pretend you've won. What would you do with it?"

He then got into the spirit of the conversation and shared his thoughts. It was a memorable moment for them:

"When he finished, he wanted to know what I'd do with the money. I told him. Well, it turned out that we not only had a lot of fun talking about how we'd spend the money, but we learned a lot about each other. I found out that he was more thoughtful and considerate of others than I'd realized. One thing he said he'd do was buy a home for his mother who is divorced. And he'd pay for his younger brother's college.

"I was really touched by that. And he was delighted that I'd give a large gift to my favorite charity—a home for abused children. It was clear from our conversation that we were both family oriented and interested in helping others. I think that's when we got serious about our relationship and started thinking about making it a permanent one."

No matter whether you've been together a short time or many years, sharing your dreams and fantasies is a way both to learn more about each other and to shape your relationship. In other words, it's one of those important ways that couples play for keeps.

Play for Keeps

Word play and sharing your dreams are not the only intimacy games you can draw on when you have a small chunk of time. In fact, it's good to have as many as possible to choose from because a particular game may be more or less appropriate for a given time or place. Clearly, for example, you shouldn't play hangman while driving in heavy traffic. And you won't want to share your dreams and fantasies while standing in a long line. That kind of conversation is meant for the two of you, not for those standing around you in line.

Make as long a list as you can of the small chunks of time you typically have as a couple. Think about the kinds of games you could use in each of them. You might want to create one or more games for specific situations. For example, the following is a game we created for the time we're sitting in an airport. It's also good for any time you're sitting side by side and don't need to have your eyes open (such as resting on a park bench).

Close your eyes and get in touch with your other senses. What do you hear? What do you smell? Describe for each other all the sounds and odors you detect. What do you feel?

This is a learning as well as a connecting exercise. For instance, we have learned that Jeanette picks up on sounds of children more quickly than Bob, while he is more sensitive to the sounds of equipment. We have also learned how much we miss when we are primarily engaging the environment with our eyes. And as always, we have experienced the bonding power of play.

10

Do It!

As university professors, we have never been enamored of the old saw, "Those who can, do; those who can't, teach." Still, it carries an important truth: knowing doesn't necessarily translate into doing. For various reasons, you may not put into practice something you know. Usually, it isn't because you *can't*. Rather, you are so caught up in the demands of the moment that it doesn't occur to you to *do* what you *know*.

Ted, who teaches communications in college, is a first-rate example:

"For years I've taught students the importance of good communication in everything from business to personal relationships. I've taught them the skills they need to be effective communicators and listeners.

"You can imagine my chagrin one day when my wife angrily said to me, 'You haven't listened to one word I've said. You don't understand what I'm telling you.' That really took me aback. Here I am an expert in communications, and Libby said I wasn't listening to her? Could she possibly be right?

"I protested at the time. But as I thought about it, I realized I probably hadn't really been *hearing* her. Oh, I'd act like I was listening, nodding occasionally to indicate my attention. But I wasn't really attending to her words or giving much thought to what she was feeling. In other words, I wasn't practicing what I preached to my students.

"I embarked right then on a program of change. I took careful note of how I communicated with Libby. I watched my style of communication with others both inside and outside of the classroom. And I'm happy to report that what I teach does really work. But you can't just know about it. You also have to practice it."

You now know a lot about couple play. The question is, are you practicing what you know? In this chapter, we want to give you a few tools that will help you achieve that end. Here are five principles to keep in mind, an admonition to follow, and a stimulus list to use.

Five Principles

Your first tool is a set of five principles that are based on the materials found in previous chapters. We offer them here as reminders for you to use as you develop your couple play. They are:

1. The enjoyment principle
2. The understanding principle
3. The memory principle
4. The anywhere and everywhere principle
5. The adventure principle

Let's review what they mean.

The Enjoyment Principle

The point of play is for you *both* to be absorbed in something that is *pure pleasure*. Note the emphasis on "both" and on "pure pleasure." It's not couple play unless you're *both* enjoying it. If one of you finds an activity boring, frightening, or repugnant, it isn't play, no matter how much the other enjoys it. If one or both of you does anything to detract from the pure pleasure of the activity, it isn't couple play any longer. And there are many ways in which couples manage to drain some or all of the joy out of their play.

This is what happened to Judy and Spenser. They shared a hobby of collecting Depression glass. They frequented antique shops in their city and wherever they traveled. As time passed, their interest grew to include other small antique items. One day a friend suggested they check the Internet site eBay. They didn't find any pieces they wanted to buy, but they realized that they could sell as well as buy. They began looking for items they could buy at a bargain price and then offer for sale on the Internet. Their hobby turned into a business effort. What began as couple play became a pursuit of profit. Visiting antique shops was no longer a purely pleasurable adventure, but a search for business opportunities.

The enjoyment principle means that you must resist anything that turns an activity from pure pleasure to another end. Don't use couple play to compete with your partner. Don't choose activities that are too costly in money or time; they'll end up causing you worry. And don't use couple play as a means to improve your physical and mental health. Certainly, these will benefit from your play. But if they are the purpose of your play, you will dilute or even destroy its value.

In other words, when you engage in couple play, really play! Enjoy yourselves. That's the point.

The Understanding Principle

Know your own and your partner's preferences for play. This principle guides your choices and intensifies your pleasure. For example, Monty told us:

> "When we plan our vacations, I research the possibilities and suggest a couple to Jessica. I know the kinds of things she likes to do, so I don't

suggest something like a float trip. She can't swim and hates water sports generally. Instead, I look for things that I think we'd both enjoy doing."

This understanding intensifies their pleasure:

"If I told Jess that I really wanted to go on a float trip, I know she'd do it. But neither of us would look forward to it. She'd be anxious, and I'd feel bad about her anxiety. So we choose things that both of us expect to enjoy. Half of the fun is the anticipation and actual experience of doing them. The other half is knowing that we're sensitive to each other's feelings and want to please each other."

In Chapter 3, you completed your play profiles. Use your findings as you plan for couple play or engage in spur-of-the-moment play. At the same time, keep in mind that your play profiles will change. You may have a strong preference for physical play now, only to find yourself shifting to social or cultural play in a few years. We suggest that you periodically reconstruct your play profiles—perhaps every three to five years. Keep your understanding current.

The Memory Principle

Recall past times of couple play that were particularly pleasurable. This principle yields three benefits. First, it helps to keep your mind in the play mode. As Lynn, a young mother, pointed out, thinking about past experiences is one way to break through the clamor of demands that consume your attention:

"During our premarital counseling, the priest told us that when we had children our lives would change dramatically. I didn't really believe him at the time, but he was right—I had no idea how demanding and exhausting motherhood would be. Often the last thing on my mind is how Joel and I can have fun together—that is, until we recall some of the fun times we've had in the past. Then I want more of the same."

Second, remembering allows you to delight in those special moments again and again. And as Lynn found, this can bring relief from the stresses of everyday life:

"I was bone-weary one evening and feeling anxious about all I had to do the next day. I complained to Joel about how hectic life seemed. He agreed. 'What a contrast,' he said, 'to the time when we cruised the Caribbean.' Of course, that was before we had kids. We'd felt so pampered and so free. And you know what? Our memories didn't make me feel envious of the past. They just left me feeling relaxed and renewed. I went to bed that night with fewer worries about the next day."

Third, remembering past times of enjoyment may bring to mind something you want to do again. Joel and Lynn determined after that night that they would plan another cruise in the near future. "My mom has volunteered to stay with the kids whenever we want to get away," Lynn said, "so we're aiming for Alaska in June."

We use the memory of past fun times with couples who feel like their relationship has bottomed out. We ask them, "What was going on when you were happy together? How did you behave with each other? What did you enjoy doing together?" We have found that sometimes a troubled relationship can be revived if a couple reverts to earlier forms of behavior and play. If it worked for you in the past, it might work for you now.

The Anywhere and Everywhere Principle

Opportunities for couple play abound. The anywhere and every-where principle reminds us that couple play doesn't require something exotic or expensive or time consuming. No matter how limited your resources, you can always find ways to play together. The principle also reminds us that play opportunities are not confined to certain times or places. You can incorporate play into most activities and situations. As psychiatrist William Betcher succinctly put it, "The first place to look for ideas and opportunities to play is exactly where you are."[1] Whether you play or don't play, then, is more likely a result of your attitudes and decisions rather than circumstances.

Consider the following scenario. It's typical of many couples we have worked with who complain that they have little time for play.

The couple begins their Saturday with household chores. She cleans while he works in the yard. He comes in for an early lunch. She doesn't want to stop what she's doing, so he eats alone. She has a light lunch later. After they finish their household chores, they do their grocery shopping. They drive silently to the store and say little to each other as they each take half the grocery list and secure the needed items. After a silent drive home, they put the groceries away. A neighbor drops in and talks with them about a problem with the homeowners association. Various other tasks and phone calls consume the rest of the afternoon.

The couple then discusses dinner. They spend a good deal of time debating whether to go out or eat in. Once they decide to eat out, neither wants to make a decision about where. They finally settle on a nearby Italian restaurant, their default place whenever they can't make up their minds. He watches a football game on the giant television while they eat. They go home and he turns on the television while she gets caught up on a few odds and ends. Eventually, she joins him to watch a program. At the program's end, it is time for bed.

This scenario is by no means unrealistic. And it's a good illustration of how many opportunities are missed by couples who say they have little time for play. Can you point out the many opportunities this couple missed to play together? How could they have altered their activities to put more fun into their Saturday?

The Adventure Principle

Maintain surprise and anticipation in your relationship. We were reminded of this principle when we heard a minister begin a wedding service with these words: "Beloved, marriage is an adventure in the most intimate of human relationships." The word *adventure* caught our attention. We love it. Every intimate relationship should have an element of adventure, times of surprise and anticipation.

We say "an element" because, realistically, no relationship is an unrelenting experience of any one thing. If you're in it for the long haul, you will have times when you're bored, when you argue, when you don't like your partner, and when you fantasize about someone else. Such times are normal. Yet for a sizzling, to-die-for relationship, you must also have times of surprise and anticipation. There must be a strand of adventure in your relationship.

Couple play is a primary source of adventure. For example, a man married for twenty-two years listed the following as some of the adventures he'd had with his wife:

- Our honeymoon
- The birth of our children
- Moving across the country to start new careers
- Our first cruise
- The time she read a book about sex and initiated some new sexual techniques with me
- Our first trip to Paris
- Working together to remodel our house

Note how many of the items involved some form of couple play. Also note how many of them refer to first-time experiences. To keep the adventure in your relationship, keep expanding your repertoire of play by trying new things. Variety really is the spice in a lifelong relationship.

An Admonition

Our admonition is simple but crucial: *schedule your couple play*. This isn't a substitute for spur-of-the-moment play. But don't make the mistake of having all or even most of your play be spur-of-the-moment. And don't reserve it only for those times when all other demands and responsibilities are met. Scheduled play is the most effective way for busy people (which includes all of us) to bring more play into their lives. It assures that play will be an integral part of your lives rather than an afterthought.

Moreover, when you schedule couple play, it's easier to say no to conflicting demands. In our view, couple play is a legitimate reason for saying no to requests for your time. On more than one occasion, we have turned down an invitation to speak because it conflicted with a scheduled time of couple play. "We're sorry," we simply say, "but we're not free that night."

To effectively schedule couple play, you will need time-management skills and a calendar. The time-management skills will enable you to make room for couple play. The calendar will serve as a reminder.

Develop Time-Management Skills

Is it possible to meet the demands and responsibilities you now face in less time than you are currently taking? For a surprising number of couples, we find the answer is yes. It's a matter of learning and using some basic time-management skills. We have identified six such skills that give couples more time for each other:[2]

1. Make a list of what you need and want to do.
2. Set priorities.
3. Put time limits on activities.
4. Do tasks simultaneously whenever possible.
5. Avoid time traps.
6. Get help.

Make a List of What You Need and Want to Do Most people we know have more things they need and want to do than they can easily keep in their heads. We find that when we make a list, we are more effective and efficient. When we don't make a list, we often find ourselves retracing our steps to do something we had forgotten. A businesswoman put it well:

> "I write down both my business and domestic tasks for each day. When I didn't do this, I had all these things swirling around in my head and I would keep thinking of things I had forgotten to do. When I found my mind wandering during sex, I knew I had to do something to get things in order. A daily list is the answer. It's made a difference in how much and how well we play."

Set Priorities The items on your list are not equally important. Your list includes both what you *need* to do and what you *want* to do. You may need to keep a doctor's appointment. Many other matters that people talk about as "need to" are actually "want to," where "want to" means either "I would enjoy" or "I believe I ought to." In those terms, is spring housecleaning on a particular day a need or a want? If you want to do some spring housecleaning and also want to take a long walk together, which one has priority if you don't have time for both?

Thinking about the items on your list in terms of "need" versus "want" helps prioritize them. And setting priorities helps you feel comfortable when lower-priority items do not get done on a given day. Just a reminder: avoid consistently placing couple play among the lower-priority items on your list.

Put Time Limits on Activities Have you ever had this kind of experience?

> "We had a dinner party for three other couples we'd recently met. Everything was going really well. We were enjoying the conversation

and also looking forward to later when we would be alone and could make love. It turned out that one of the couples were night owls. The others left, but they stayed until 1:00 in the morning! When they left, we were too exhausted to even clean up, much less make love."

At some point the hosts could have *gently* let the night owls know that the time for socializing had ended. Whether it's a work or social situation, you need to put time limits on activities. Decide in advance how much time you want to give to something, and decide how you will make your limit known if that becomes necessary. For example, we suggested that the night owls be told, "It's been so much fun having you over, but it's way past our bedtime. Let's continue this conversation at another time."

It isn't rude to put time limits on activities. It's a way to safeguard one of your most precious possessions—time. In many cases, you can let the limit be known in advance. For instance, if you get a phone call from a friend who typically drones on and on, you can tell the friend upfront how much time you have to talk. If you go to a party, you can tell the host and hostess what time you must leave. We once served on a committee whose meetings began at 7:00 P.M. and often lasted until 10 or 11. A friend who was asked to join the committee agreed but said at the outset that he would only stay until 9:00 P.M. And when the clock struck 9, he left—no matter what was happening!

Do Tasks Simultaneously Whenever Possible   "I can only do one thing at a time." This may be an effective way to avoid responding to a request when you're already involved in another task, but it isn't strictly true. In fact, we can often do more than one thing at a time. So double up whenever possible and you'll free up more time for couple play.

We say "whenever possible" because some situations require your full attention. Driving is one. Talking to someone on the telephone who is troubled and needs you to listen carefully is another. On the other hand, with long cords or cordless telephones, less serious conversations on the telephone can often be combined with another task. For example, Gwen and her fiancé had a date to go ice skating. Before they left, she had to clean up her breakfast dishes and write a few checks for bills that were due. As she started on the dishes, her phone rang. It was her friend Suzanne. Gwen was still talking to Suzanne when her fiancé arrived for their date. And he was aggravated when she insisted on finishing her chores before they left.

Gwen made two mistakes. First, she could have put time limits on the telephone conversation. She could have called Suzanne back later or limited the conversation to a few minutes. Second, she could have done the dishes and written her checks while talking. Suzanne was not troubled; she and Gwen were simply catching up. Doing her tasks while talking would have given her more time to play and would have saved her from having to deal with an irritated partner.

Avoid Time Traps A *time trap* is any behavior that needlessly wastes time. Typical time traps include procrastination, perfectionism, and prolonged decision making. Procrastination is likely when you face a task you dislike. You can procrastinate by piddling with other things as you try to avoid the task. If you have a problem with procrastination, agree to reward yourself with something fun as soon as the onerous task is complete.

Perfectionism may be more difficult to deal with. If you are a perfectionist, you may spend an inordinate amount of time doing your work, caring for your home, getting dressed to go out, and so forth. Try to think in terms of priorities. Is it more valuable to have your home spotless or to spend time with your partner? Is it better to spend great gulps of time shopping for the perfect gift at the best possible price or to use that time for couple play? Learn to compromise your perfectionist standards. Your relationship will be richer for it.

Finally, we dealt with prolonged decision making in the last chapter. If you find yourselves wasting time trying to make a decision, turn the process into a game. Rescue those decision-making minutes from frustration and irritation and use them to enjoy one another.

Get Help   The service industry has expanded to the point where, if you can afford it, you need not do much of anything except work and play. In most places, you can hire people to clean your house, take care of your yard, come to the house to service the cars and groom the dog, do your shopping, and deliver gourmet meals seven days a week. And you can deposit most of your income directly and have most of your bills paid automatically at your bank.

Although you probably don't use all of these services, they are available. The point is, if you can afford it, why not get some help and free up more time for couple play? If the idea of spending money in this way bothers you, ask yourselves: *What have we gained if we save money but don't have time to enjoy each other?* It might also help to put an altruistic spin on the matter by reminding yourselves how much you are helping someone else by providing that person employment. The bottom line is, getting help you can afford isn't wasting money; it's freeing up time for couple play.

Keep a Calendar

Your calendar probably includes such things as business responsibilities, family gatherings, doctor and dental appointments, scheduled social events, and regular activities such as a concert series or workouts at a health club. We urge you to schedule couple play on your calendar as well. Joel and Lynn found this essential after they became parents:

> "For a while, parenthood put an end to our couple play. Between work and taking care of a home and a baby, we found ourselves using up every minute of every day. We didn't think we had time for play, and it was stressing us both. So one day we sat down and penciled in a 'fun time' on our calendar each week. You know what? We found that

we could make the time. But if we didn't schedule it, if we didn't plan for it, it just didn't happen."

Children aren't the only source of demand in our lives; childless couples also complain of demanding schedules and too little time. The point is, every couple needs to control their calendar. If you don't, others will. And they won't be scheduling play time for you.

You need not have fixed plans in order to reserve time for couple play. Simply write "date night" on your calendar and fill in the details later. Some couples even schedule sex. If you resist thinking that sex should always be a spontaneous coming together of two people in heat, keep in mind the words of a busy wife: "Scheduled sex is much better than no sex."

Another objection to scheduled sex is "What if I'm not in the mood?" This can happen. If it does, do something else; you've still reserved the time for couple play. Knowing that you've scheduled sex for that evening, however, may keep it in your thoughts throughout the day and put you in the mood by evening. You may or may not want to include sex on your calendar. But you should include various other kinds of couple play. Having it on the calendar will keep you from scheduling something else, give you a reason to turn down other requests, and ensure that you give ample time to couple play.

A Stimulus List: 101 Ways for Couples to Play

"What shall we do tonight?" "How can we expand our play repertoire?" "What can we do that's new and different for us?" These are questions that couples raise repeatedly. The following list will help you address the questions. Many of the activities have been mentioned in previous chapters and range from the simple to the complex. They are in no particular order, and you won't find all of them appealing. Their main purpose is to stimulate your thinking and trigger additional ideas about ways you can have fun together. Review the list whenever your couple play needs a new injection of vigor.

1. Plan a vacation to Vienna or Venice or another place that you prefer and can afford.
2. Join a coed volleyball team.
3. Invite the neighbors over for a glass of wine.
4. Take a shower or bubble bath together.
5. Tell each other a new joke every day for two weeks.
6. Don your waterproof gear and go for a walk in the rain.
7. Spend Saturday morning in bed—making love, reading the paper, watching TV, talking about your fantasies.
8. Throw a "Let's Celebrate Today" party.
9. Write and mail a love letter to each other.
10. Plant a flower garden.
11. Go water or snow skiing.
12. Lie in the grass and describe what you see in the clouds.
13. Take a gourmet cooking class.
14. Go on a date and pretend it's your first.
15. Take a hot air balloon ride.
16. Attend a concert.
17. Browse a local farmers market.
18. Choose a classic movie and invite friends over for an interactive film night (à la *The Rocky Horror Picture Show*).
19. Plan a vacation around art museums or roller coasters or anything else that catches your fancy.
20. Have a "junk food" dinner.
21. Play video games at the mall.
22. Fly a kite.
23. Have phone sex when you're apart.
24. Take karate lessons.
25. Learn to jitterbug.
26. Work a challenging jigsaw puzzle.

27. Surf the Internet for sites with jokes and other humor.
28. Have sex someplace other than your bed.
29. Park the car on Lovers' Lane and make out.
30. Assume the identity of a famous couple for the day.
31. Give each other a foot massage.
32. Play footsies at a restaurant.
33. Create a personal and romantic nickname for your partner.
34. Build a sandcastle or a snowman.
35. Toast marshmallows in the fireplace.
36. Go for a hike.
37. Play mah-jongg with another couple.
38. Sing love songs to each other.
39. Celebrate "Hug Day," giving each other a hug every time your paths cross.
40. Go backpacking.
41. Go horseback riding.
42. Take up stamp collecting.
43. Dust off your musical instruments from high school days and play duets.
44. Take an aerobics class.
45. Plan a weekend love feast at a nearby motel.
46. Make a point of visiting different coffee houses when you travel and keep a journal of your findings about the coffee, the ambience, the conversation, and so on.
47. Cook an exotic ethnic dinner together.
48. Watch the sunset and talk about your dreams.
49. Build a bonfire on the beach and tell ghost stories.
50. Take turns planning mystery dates where all you tell your partner is what to wear.
51. Attend a performance by a local theatrical group.
52. Play miniature golf.
53. Go bicycling.
54. Take a walk through the autumn leaves.

55. Do yoga together.
56. Eat out at a different restaurant each night for a week.
57. Take turns reading a book to each other.
58. Become amateur stargazers.
59. Whisper a love message at an unexpected moment.
60. Enjoy past experiences by going through your photo albums.
61. Write the story of how you met and fell in love.
62. Take a cruise.
63. Go snorkeling or kayaking.
64. Borrow the kids' equipment and blow bubbles in the backyard.
65. Take an afternoon off and go on a picnic.
66. Spend a day at an amusement or water park.
67. Attend a professional sports event.
68. Go whitewater rafting.
69. Do four things that you think will increase the romance in your relationship.
70. Have a few couples over for a potluck dinner.
71. Turn on some Sousa and march through the house.
72. Try a sport you've never done together—bowling, golf, tennis, or swimming, for example.
73. Write a limerick or song that celebrates your partner.
74. Go to the Internet, type "games" in a search engine, find three games you've not played, and try them.
75. Go to a local pond and feed bread crumbs to the ducks.
76. Join a local theatrical group.
77. Play strip poker.
78. Start a book discussion group.
79. Take up photography.
80. The next time you take a motor trip, search for license plates from every state.
81. Read a book on sexual techniques and positions and try anything that looks like fun to you.

82. Run through the sprinklers in your backyard.
83. Turn a room or part of one into your couple play area.
84. Hide loves messages in your partner's pockets.
85. Visit a zoo, aquarium, or planetarium.
86. Spend a Saturday morning looking for treasures at local garage sales.
87. Host a square dance in your garage or on your patio.
88. Visit the wineries or microbreweries in your city or state.
89. Take a music or an art appreciation class.
90. Swing, slide, and roller skate at the playground.
91. Sit on a park bench and make up stories about the passersby.
92. Start a collection that you both enjoy.
93. Surprise your partner with a bouquet of flowers.
94. Make homemade ice cream or fudge.
95. Go fishing.
96. Work the Sunday crossword puzzle together.
97. Organize a neighborhood street dance and barbeque.
98. Window shop at some exclusive stores.
99. Attend a poetry reading.
100. Once a month, participate in an event that you discovered in your newspaper's weekend section.
101. Do something unexpected for each other.

Play for Keeps

Just say yes. Do it!

Notes

Chapter 1

1. Paul Roberts, "Goofing Off," *Psychology Today*, July/August 1995, pp. 34–42.

2. Jeanette C. Lauer and Robert H. Lauer, *Til Death Do Us Part: A Study and Guide to Long-Term Marriage* (New York: Harrington Park Press, 1986).

3. Carolyn J. Gard, "Humor Helps," *Current Health*, April/May 1998, pp. 22–23.

Chapter 2

1. Jeffrey Moussaieff Masson, *When Elephants Weep: The Emotional Life of Animals* (New York: Dell, 1995), pp. 124ff; Robert R. Provine, "Laughter," *American Scientist*, January/February 1996, pp. 38–48.

2. Shannon Brownlee, "The Case for Frivolity: Play Isn't Just Fun," *U.S. News & World Report*, 3 February 1997, pp. 45–48.

3. M. Sayer Saunders and A. Goodale, "The Relationship Between Playfulness and Coping in Preschool Children," *American Journal of Occupational Therapy*, March/April 1999, pp. 221–26.

4. Norman Cousins, "Proving the Power of Laughter," *Psychology Today*, vol. 23, 1989, pp. 22–25; Carolyn J. Gard, "Humor Helps," *Current Health*, April/May 1998, pp. 22–23.

5. Avner Ziv, "Humor's Role in Married Life," *Humor: International Journal of Humor Research*, no. 1 (1988), pp. 223–29.

6. Leslie A. Baxter, "Forms and Functions of Intimate Play in Personal Relationships," *Human Communication Research*, March 1992, pp. 336–63.

7. William Betcher, *Intimate Play* (New York: Viking, 1987), p. 83.

Chapter 3

1. This is reported in greater detail in Robert H. Lauer and Jeanette C. Lauer, *Marriage and Family: The Quest for Intimacy* (fourth edition) (New York: McGraw-Hill, 2000), pp. 127–28.

2. James M. Honeycutt and Renee Brown, "Did You Hear the One About?: Typological and Spousal Differences in the Planning of Jokes and Sense of Humor in Marriage," *Communication Quarterly*, summer 1998, pp. 342–56; Bernice Kanner, "It's a Laugh," *American Demographics*, April 1998, p. 17; Robert R. Provine, *Laughter: A Scientific Investigation* (New York: Viking, 2000), pp. 27–32.

Chapter 4

1. In *Intimate Play* (pp. 287ff), William Betcher discusses the differences between intimate play and destructive games from a psychiatric point of view, noting both the conscious and unconscious processes at work.

2. Lenore Terr, M.D., *Beyond Love and Work: Why Adults Need to Play* (New York: Scribner, 1999), p. 29.

3. See Chapter 6 in our book *The Ties That Bind: Growing Together in Your Marriage and Your Faith* (Nashville, TN: Upper Room Books, 2002).

4. Deborah Tannen, *You Just Don't Understand: Women and Men in Conversation* (New York: William Morrow, 1990), pp. 89–91.

5. Lewis Carroll, *Alice's Adventures in Wonderland* (New York: New American Library, 1960), pp. 66–74.

6. *Ibid.,* p. 73.

7. Arlene Modica Matthews, *Why Did I Marry You, Anyway?* (Boston: Houghton Mifflin, 1988), p. 91.

Chapter 5

1. Viktor E. Frankl, *Man's Search for Meaning* (Boston: Beacon Press, 1962), p. 42.

2. See, for example, David G. Myers, *Social Psychology* (fourth edition) (New York: McGraw-Hill, 1993), Chapter 4.

3. "Laughter IS Good for Your Heart, According to a New University of Maryland Medical Center Study," *University of Maryland Medical News*, news release, 15 November 2000.

4. William J. Lederer, *Creating a Good Relationship* (New York: W.W. Norton & Company, 1984), p. 57.

Chapter 6

1. If you're familiar with the Myers-Briggs Type Indicator or the Keirsey Temperament Sorter, you will recognize this as a descrip-

tion of two types of personalities, the P and the J. For more information, see: Otto Kroeger and Janet M. Thuesen, *Type Talk: The 16 Personality Types That Determine How We Live, Love, and Work* (New York: Dell Publishing, 1988); David Keirsey and Marilyn Bates, *Please Understand Me: Character & Temperament Types* (Del Mar, CA: Prometheus Nemesis Book Company, 1984).

2. Harold H. Bloomfield, M.D., and Robert B. Kory, *Inner Joy: New Strategies for Adding Pleasure to Your Life* (New York: A Jove Book, 1980), p. 68.

3. Kathleen Fischer Hart and Thomas N. Hart, *The First Two Years of Marriage: Foundations for a Life Together* (New York: Paulist Press, 1983), p. 62.

Chapter 7

1. R. William Betcher, "Intimate Play and Marital Adaptation," *Psychiatry*, February 1981, p. 13.

2. Richard A. Mackey and Bernard A. O'Brien, *Lasting Marriages: Men and Women Growing Together* (Westport, CN: Praeger, 1995), p. 51.

3. See, for example, Lauer and Lauer, *Til Death Do Us Part*; John Gottman, "What Makes Marriage Work?" *Psychology Today*, March/April 1994, pp. 38–43; and Howard Markman, Scott Stanley, and Susan L. Blumberg, *Fighting for Your Marriage* (San Francisco: Jossey-Bass, 1994).

4. Ted L. Huston, Susan M. McHale, and Ann C. Crouter, "When the Honeymoon's Over: Changes in the Marriage Relationship Over the First Year," in Robin Gilmour and Steve Duck, eds., *The Emerging Field of Personal Relationships* (Hillsdale, NJ: Lawrence Erlbaum Associates, 1986).

5. Susan Sprecher and Kathleen McKinney, *Sexuality* (Newbury Park, CA: Sage, 1993), p. 100.

6. Betcher, "Intimate Play and Marital Adaptation," p. 20.

7. Edith Wharton, *The Age of Innocence* (New York: Charles Scribner's Sons, 1920), p. 84.

8. Michael Balder, "You've Lost That Lovin' Feeling," *Tikkun*, March/April 1998, p. 12.

Chapter 8

1. John H. Leith, *Basic Christian Doctrine* (Louisville, KY: Westminster/John Knox Press, 1993), p. 72.

2. Philip Goldberg, *The Babinski Reflex* (Los Angeles: Jeremy P. Tarcher, Inc., 1990), pp. 93–96.

3. Robert Epstein, "Capturing Creativity," *Psychology Today*, July/August 1996, p. 41.

Chapter 9

1. Paul Roberts, *Goofing Off*, p. 35.

2. David G. Myers, *Social Psychology* (fourth edition), pp. 165–66, 525–28.

3. Kathleen Norris, *The Quotidian Mysteries* (New York: Paulist Press, 1998), p. 74.

4. *Ibid.,* p. 76.

5. *Twelfth Night*, Act I, Scene 1.

6. Rebecca Abrams, *The Playful Self: Why Women Need Play in Their Lives* (London: Fourth Estate, 1997), p. 202.

Chapter 10

1. Betcher, *Intimate Play*, p. 307.

2. Jeanette C. Lauer and Robert H. Lauer, *Intimacy on the Run: Staying Close When So Much Keeps You Apart* (Nashville, TN: Dimensions for Living, 1996), pp. 46–50.

Resources

IF YOU'D LIKE some more ideas about how to keep your relationship sizzling, we recommend the following:

Books

Betcher, William, M.D. *Intimate Play: Creating Romance in Everyday Life.* New York: Viking, 1987. A seminal work on couple play. Out of print, but you may be able to find it used or in your local library.

Godek, Gregory J. P. *1001 Ways to Be Romantic.* Naperville, IL: Sourcebooks, 1999. As the title says, 1001 ways to add fun and sizzle to your relationship.

Hart, Kathleen Fischer, and Thomas N. Hart. *The First Two Years of Marriage.* New York: Paulist Press, 1983. Good insights on various aspects of marriage, including the "lighter side."

Lauer, Robert H., and Jeanette C. Lauer. *Marriage and Family: The Quest for Intimacy.* Fourth edition. New York: McGraw-Hill, 2000.

What can we say? One of our favorite books. Covers all facets of intimacy, with practical suggestions in each chapter.

Mackey, Richard A., and Bernard A. O'Brien. *Lasting Marriages: Men and Women Growing Together.* Westport, CT: Praeger, 1995. Shows how couples maintain a great relationship throughout the years of marriage.

Markman, Howard, Scott Stanley, and Susan L. Blumberg. *Fighting for Your Marriage.* San Francisco: Jossey-Bass, 1994. Helpful, practical advice, including a chapter on increasing your fun together.

Partow, Cameron, and Donna Partow. *Families That Play Together Stay Together.* Minneapolis, MN: Bethany House, 1996. Written for families, but has many good ideas for couple play as well.

Pines, Ayala Malach. *Falling in Love: Why We Choose the Lovers We Choose.* New York: Routledge, 1999. Helps you understand why you came together, an important basis for fashioning a more playful relationship.

Terr, Lenore. *Beyond Love and Work: Why Adults Need to Play.* New York: Scribner's, 1999. A psychiatrist's explanation of why we all need to play, in case you or your partner aren't yet fully convinced.

Internet Sites

www.humorproject.com Use it for daily laughs together.

www.wholefamily.com Click on "marriage center" for both light and serious treatments of various issues and challenges.

www.youmarriedhim.com Use for humor and for ideas for couple play (check the "romance igniters").

Index